UNDERSTANDING FAITH

# Understanding Judaism

# UNDERSTANDING FAITH

SERIES EDITOR: PROFESSOR FRANK WHALING

*Also published:*
Understanding Islam, Professor David Kerr

*Forthcoming titles:*
Understanding Christianity, Gilleasbuig Macmillan
Understanding Hinduism, Frank Whaling
Understanding Sikhism, W. Owen Cole

# UNDERSTANDING FAITH

SERIES EDITOR: FRANK WHALING

# UNDERSTANDING JUDAISM

## Rabbi Jeremy Rosen

*Professor and Chairman
of the Faculty for Comparative Religion, Antwerp, Belgium
and Director, YAKAR Educational Centre, London, UK*

DUNEDIN ACADEMIC PRESS
EDINBURGH

Published by
Dunedin Academic Press Ltd
Hudson House
8 Albany Street
Edinburgh EH1 3QB
Scotland

ISBN 1 903765 30 7

*British Library Cataloguing in Publication Data*
A catalogue record for this book is available from the British Library

Typeset by Patty Rennie Production, Portsoy
Printed in Great Britain by Cromwell Press

# Contents

# Dateline

| BCE | JEWISH | DATES | BOOKS | NON-JEWISH |
|---|---|---|---|---|
| | | | | *Ur* |
| 2000 | ABRAHAM | | | *Gilgamesh Epic* |
| | | | | *Hammurabi* |
| | | | | |
| | | | | *Akhenaten* |
| 1500 | | | | *Hyksos* |
| | MOSES | | Books of Moses | |
| | | | *Joshua* | |
| | | | | |
| | | | *Judges* | |
| 1000 | DAVID | | *Samuel* | |
| | Solomon | 900 | | |
| | | | *Kings* | *Assyria* |
| | ISRAEL destroyed | 722 | *Prophets* | |
| | | | | *Babylon* |
| | JUDEA and 1st | 586 | | *Nebuchadnezzar* |
| | TEMPLE destroyed | | | |
| 500 | Return | | | *Buddha* |
| | Zerubavel | | | *Confucius* |
| | EZRA & NEHEMIAH | | | |
| | | 332 | | *Socrates* |
| | SHIMON HATSADIK | | | *Alexander* |

| CE | JEWISH | DATES | BOOKS | NON-JEWISH | |
|----|--------|-------|-------|------------|---|
| | | 168 | *Apocrypha* | | |
| | JUDAH MACCABEE | | *Maccabees* | | |
| | HEROD | | *Qumran* | | |
| | 2nd TEMPLE destroyed | 70 | *Hechalot* | | |
| | Bar Cochba | 132–135 | *Shiur Koma* | | |
| | R. Yehuda HaNassi | 170–217 | Mishna | | |
| | | 311 | | *Constantine* | |
| | | 350 | Jerusalem Talmud | *Nicaea* | |
| 500 | Ravina and Rav Ashi | | Babylonian Talmud | *Justinian Code* | |
| | | | *Sefer Bahir* | | |
| | | | *Sefer Yetzira* | *Mohammad* | |
| | Geonim | | | *Omar* | |
| | Saadyah Gaon | 882–942 | | | |
| 1000 | RASHI | 1040–1105 | | *1st Crusade* | |
| | MAIMONIDES | 1135–1204 | *Mishne Torah* | *2nd Crusade* | |
| | Nachmanides | 1194–1270 | | | |
| | Abulafia | 1240–1292 | Zohar | | |
| | Moses De Leon | 1250–1305 | | | |
| | | | | *Black Death* | |
| | | 1492 | | *Spanish Expulsion* | |
| 1500 | JOSEF KARO | 1488–1575 | *Shulchan Aruch* | *Columbus* | |
| | R. Moses Cordovero | 1522–1570 | | *Luther* | 1517 |
| | ISAAC LURIA (ARIZAL) | 1534–1572 | | | |
| | Sabbatai Zevi | 1626–1678 | | *Chmielnicki* | 1648 |
| | BAAL SHEM TOV | 1700–1760 | | | |
| | GAON OF VILNA | 1720–1797 | | | |
| | | | | *Napoleon* | |
| | | 1904 | | *Bayliss libel* | |
| | | 1942 | | *Holocaust* | |
| 2000 | Israel | 1948 | | | |

# List of Illustrations

All illustrations are taken from the *Routledge Atlas of Jewish History*, 6th Edition, © Sir Martin Gilbert, published by Routledge 2002. ISBN 0 415 28150 4 (PB) and ISBN 0 415 28149 0 (HB). Please visit their website www.tandf.co.uk for further details.

# Preface

As anyone who loves knows, impartiality is incredibly difficult. I love Judaism. As a result I am very conscious of how commitment can distort. However, cold 'objective' analysis can distort too and academic life is as full of human bias as are other areas of human activity. I want to present Judaism in as objective a light as I can, but I must make it clear that I am describing a living religion and I am looking at its history through its own eyes.

I lecture at the Faculteit voor Vergelijkende Godsdienstwetenschappen (The Faculty for Comparative Religion) in Antwerp, Belgium. It is a remarkable little institution not because it insists that students study a range of religions, but because it also insists that religions can only be taught by someone practising and committed to the religion he or she is teaching. I believe the benefits of this approach far outweigh any possible deficiencies. Too often Judaism is described by those who are not passionately committed to its way of life.

My work in Comparative Religion convinces me that all religions share many basic concepts and ideas and that each one tends to exaggerate or overemphasise certain aspects to the detriment of others. I believe that these differences owe more to cultural and political forces than to genuinely spiritual ones. I do not understand how a religion can excuse taking life simply on abstract or theological grounds. Yes indeed, Moses gave such instructions, but that was nearly 4,000 years ago. I find it disturbing that in too many parts of the modern world religion and violence seem to go together. Yet I can no more hold religion itself to blame any more than football for its hooligans.

I know how difficult it is to categorise religions with their different extremes and schisms and variations. Talk about 'Christianity' or 'Islam' is not very helpful, unless one is much more specific, because there are so many variations, so many sects and divisions that are almost as implacably opposed to each other as they are to outsiders. So it is with Judaism. Small as it is, perhaps no more than twelve million, Judaism is divided into all sorts of different segments, religious, secular, and national. I will try to explain the variations as best I can.

In my style of writing I try to reflect a Jewish world outlook. So I do not refer to BC 'Before Christ' or AD 'Anno Domini' because such terms are irrelevant to Jews who do not ascribe to Jesus any particular status above that of any other human. Instead, I talk about BCE 'Before the Common Era' or CE

'Common Era'. When I talk about the bible I mean specifically the Jewish bible. Christians may call it the Old Testament, but that is offensive to Jews implying, as it does, that the 'Old' has been superseded by the 'New'. I confess that in my historical and theological overviews I have taken a very personal view as to which events or personalities I have selected over the 3,500 years I cover. But I hope I have selected the essential and the crucial features.

My transliterations are in general based on the Modern Hebrew pronunciation. This is the version used by most Hebrew-speaking Jews today, even though most Orthodox Jews in the Diaspora, in the realms of liturgy, continue to use the old Ashkenazi pronunciations that varied from country to country in Europe. You can still identify a Jew from the way he or she pronounces Hebrew. In truth, the most accurate pronunciation of Hebrew is that of the Yemenite Jews, but theirs is both more complicated and more Arabic, and therefore harder on the western ear. However, with regard to familiar biblical names, it would be too misleading for me to talk about Moshe instead of Moses or Yitschak instead of Isaac, so I retain the familiar usage. The eighth letter of the Hebrew alphabet is the guttural *chet*. Academically, there are various ways of indicating it in written form. I use '*ch*'. As in Hebrew there is no equivalent of the English *ch* sound, you should assume that all *ch*'s in Hebrew words are guttural.

God is one of the problems in talking about religion because the term means different things to different people and it is very difficult anyway to know what a person really thinks. In English there is only one word, God. We use anthropomorphisms like Lord, King of Kings, Judge, and so on. But in Hebrew there are seven biblical names for God. YHVH is the senior name. It is often pronounced Jehovah, but we have lost the original that anyway was uttered only in the Temple. Jews do not try to replicate it nowadays, substituting Adonai, My Master, in ritual situations and HaShem, The Name, in mundane conversation. But other names indicate the multifaceted way Jews have come to understand the uniquely single Divine. But there is no translation that does justice to the nuances of Yah, El, Elohim, Shaddai, Tsevaot, Adonai and, of course, YHVH. In English one name covers all, inaccurately.

Finally, I apologise in advance for any offence. None is intended either to Jews or Gentiles. I am trying to describe as objectively and as accurately as I can, but as J.C. Collingwood said, 'There is no such thing as History. There are only historians.'

In the opening chapter I am going to give a bird's-eye view of Jewish history, interlinking with the major civilisations it came into contact with. We are going to follow a longer thread of historical continuity against a wider range of differing cultures than any other civilisation. We will start in Babylon 4,000 years ago and encounter Egypt, Persia, Greece, Rome, the Christian Holy Roman Empires, Islam, Europe, the Middle East, and America. Please refer to the dateline to get your bearings and to keep them.

                                                                        J.R.

# Chapter 1

# An Historical Overview

## THE BEGINNINGS

The origins of the Jewish tradition go back nearly 4,000 years. There are early Babylonian poems from that time, the *Enuma Elish*, the *Epic of Creation*, and the *Epic of Gilgamesh*, which includes a story of a great flood. The first documented legal system we have was drawn up by Hammurabi, the king and lawgiver who lived in the area we now call Iraq, 3,700 years ago. The two major powers in the Middle East at that time were Egypt and, to use a generic name, Babylon. It is to these two crucibles of human culture we look for the origins of what is reflected in the biblical tradition.

Archaeological evidence reinforces the authenticity of much of the background described in the Bible. Biblical narrative about Abraham does not prove his existence, but a great deal of the detail has been corroborated. Migration northward up the valleys of the Tigris and Euphrates was 'donkey driven' towards Haran and then dropped southward through what is now Syria to the Jordan valley or the coastal plain towards Egypt. Only the rich could afford a shorter overland direct route, which required camels. Excavations at Ebla and Ras Shamra offer striking correspondences with Hebrew life and culture at the time.

The Tel El Amarna documents, found in Egypt, are diplomatic despatches that describe a Middle East in a state of upheaval in about 1400 BCE. An invading people called the Hapiru may or may not be identified with the Hebrews. Changes in Egypt in the second half of that millennium provide fertile ground for the events the Bible describes. The religious revolution of Akhenaten challenged the old Egyptian religious traditions before the old order was restored. The invasions of the nomadic Hyksos tribes about the same time destabilised Egyptian society before they were expelled. This resonates with the biblical narrative of one king welcoming nomads and another enslaving them.

Many Jews take the first five books of the Bible as the exact word of God revealed to Moses on Mount Sinai 3,500 years ago. Some committed Jews accept it as a valid record of a religious encounter, rather than a scientific record of objective history. Others treat it as an expression of a particular culture they are connected to.

In brief, a people that went down to Egypt as a large extended family emerged hundreds of years later as a nation structured tribally with a priest-

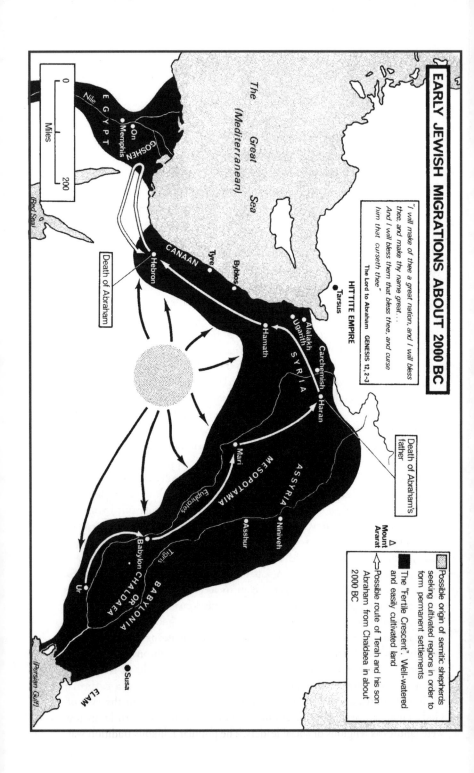

# EARLY JEWISH MIGRATIONS ABOUT 2000 BC

"I will make of thee a great nation, and I will bless thee, and make thy name great...
And I will bless them that bless thee, and curse him that curseth thee"

The Lord to Abraham  GENESIS 12, 2-3

Death of Abraham's father

Death of Abraham

Possible origin of semitic shepherds seeking cultivated regions in order to form permanent settlements

The "Fertile Crescent". Well-watered and easily cultivated land

Possible route of Terah and his son Abraham from Chaldaea in about 2000 BC

Mount Ararat

Miles
0    200

EGYPT
Nile
Memphis
On
GOSHEN
The Great Sea (Mediterranean)
Red Sea

CANAAN
Hebron
Tyre
Byblos
HITTITE EMPIRE
Tarsus

Ugarith
Alalakh
Hamath
SYRIA
Carchemish
Haran
Mari
MESOPOTAMIA
Euphrates
ASSYRIA
Asshur
Niniveh
Tigris
Babylon
CHALDAEA
BABYLONIA
Ur
Susa
ELAM
Persian Gulf

hood at the top of the social hierarchy. Under strong leadership they were welded together into a force that successfully entered the land of Canaan and settled there in about 1300 BCE.

Moses died before the crossing of the Jordan and it was Joshua, his successor, who masterminded the invasion. After the first wave of united endeavour, the tribes were left to fend for themselves. The succeeding period of the Judges was one of struggle for survival, both political and religious. Most of the time the Israelite tribes found themselves subject to alien powers and their religions. Occasional leaders emerged from different tribes who managed to galvanise support and throw off alien domination. Then after a while internal dissension weakened the fragile unity.

Very little is told in the Books of Joshua and Judges about how the religion of the people was sustained. The Judges were not described as spiritual leaders. The priesthood failed in its custodial role, and foreign deities and cults were readily adopted. Only occasional 'heroes', such as Ehud, Deborah, Gideon, Jephthah, and Samson, emerged as colourful leaders.

## THE FIRST KINGDOM AND THE TEMPLE

In approximately 1000 BCE, 3,000 years ago, the last of the Judges, Samuel (who was the most successful of them all), was pressurised by the tribes to appoint a king. He was reluctant at first because he saw this as a repudiation of divine authority. He relented, but the choice of Saul from the small tribe of Benjamin proved a failure, and so David from the dominant tribe of Judah was anointed to replace him.

Thus began the dynasty that had a crucial influence on Jewish self-expression. There is disagreement about how much David and his son Solomon extended the boundaries of their kingdom. Some doubt their existence altogether. We have enough external evidence to confirm the fact of two kingdoms that emerged after Solomon's death. Judea, the House of David, joined only by the tribe of Benjamin, was located around Jerusalem and the south. Solomon's son Rehoboam continued that dynastic line, which, with one brief interlude, would continue throughout the life of the First Kingdom.

The other ten tribes resented the centralisation and dominance of Jerusalem. Initially they asked Rehoboam to accommodate them. When he refused, they broke away and founded the Kingdom of Israel. Jeroboam, a fugitive from Solomon, came back to lead the new kingdom.

The north experienced almost continuous assassinations and changes of dynasty. Only in one case did a grandson succeed to the throne. It is hard to find one northern king about whom the scribes of the Books of Kings and Chronicles have anything good to say.

To the south, there were occasional kings who 'did good in the eyes of God', Hezekiah or Josiah, for example. More often the southern kings too were failures as religious or social leaders. The popular religious tradition was maintained by schools of prophets, itinerant charismatic leaders representing the ethical values of the *Torah*. They were in almost constant conflict with authority. The prophets represented a totally different perspective on Judaism to that of the establishment, the kings and the priests.

There were moments when the priesthood saved the day, as when they rescued Joash from Athalia. But in general, Isaiah and Jeremiah and the Minor Prophets, such as Amos and Micah ('minor' only because of the size of their written testimonies), stood in idealistic opposition to the politically and morally prevaricating authority of government. Their agenda was that political power as an end in itself was doomed to failure. Unless society was run on ethical lines it would collapse. Their complaints against contemporary religious behaviour were that it was being abused and seen as an end in itself rather than a tool for improving society and mankind.

The two kingdoms were caught in a constant round of jealous conflict and war against each other. Only occasionally did they form alliances against greater threats. These were due to external pressures, sandwiched as they were between the northern and eastern powers of Syria, then Assyria and Babylon, and to the south, the giant Egypt. These two great power zones exercised constant influence on the political and religious lives of the two Jewish kingdoms, and their archaeological artefacts provide corroborative evidence about the two 'troublesome' Jewish states.

The Assyrians regularly invaded both the North north and the South-south. Their stelae, discovered in Nineveh and Nimrud, record the victories over the Jewish kingdoms. The northern kingdom of Israel was finally destroyed by Sargon in 722 BCE. The Syrians besieged the South south too and tried to conquer it, but failed.

Assyrian policy was to remove all conquered inhabitants, scatter them throughout their Empire to ensure that they never could pose a threat in the future, and replace them with other conquered, displaced peoples. For nearly 200 years, these transplanted peoples would coexist with the southern kingdom of Judea and adopt many of their customs and traditions. In time they came to be called the Samaritans after Samaria, Omri's capital city.

Meanwhile in the south, the House of David staggered on, caught between Babylon, which had replaced Assyria as the northern power, and Egypt. Eventually in 586 BCE, after a series of conquests and exiles, Nebuchadnezzar destroyed Judea and the First Temple. In earlier conquests most of the members of the royal family and aristocracy had been taken into exile in Babylon. Finally, the remainder of the elite and the skilled workers were removed to Babylon.

The rest of the population was left behind under a Babylonian-appointed Jewish governor, Gedalia, who was assassinated by pro-Egyptian rebels. The remnant of the Judean state fled to Egypt. For the first time in some 800 years there were no Jews left in the land they regarded as theirs.

## THE BABYLONIAN EXILE

Babylonian methods of keeping the Jews together turned into a blessing in disguise. The exiles came in waves and were allowed to establish a structured Jewish society and to keep a sense of identity. The vibrant community attracted those members of the ten northern tribes who were now free to move within the Babylonian Empire. Tribal differences continued, particularly those among the priesthood. In general, the rest of the community now identified either with those loyal to the House of David or to the northern House of Joseph (or Ephraim), as it came to be called. They were now known as descendents of the House of Judea, Jews, rather than the earlier general term that the prophet Jonah had used, Hebrews.

Some fifty years after the main Babylonian exile, the Persian Empire had destroyed the successor kingdom of the Medes (this is recorded by the writing on the wall at Belshazzar's feast). The Persian king Cyrus now had an Empire stretching from India in the east to the Mediterranean in the west. He had an interest in establishing a sympathetic state as a buffer between him and the Western powers. According to the Bible, he handed back the captured temple vessels and allowed Zerubavel, a Judean prince, to lead the return of a small advance party to Jerusalem.

The returning Jews were faced with the resistance of the Samaritans. Their leader Sanballat argued that they had no right to return. They actively fought the rebuilding of the Temple. It was only when Nehemiah, a prominent politician, and Ezra the Scribe, a spiritual giant, combined to lead a second return in 458 BCE that the renewal of Jewish life around Jerusalem succeeded. Meanwhile, most Jews stayed behind in Babylon under the Persians.

From this moment on Jewish life would always be diffused. Most lived in Babylon or Egypt and set up their own communities with their own leadership. Although the rebuilt Temple was looked upon by nearly everyone as the spiritual centre, there continued to be differences of practice, ideology and character which added both variety and conflict to Jewish life thereafter.

## EZRA AND RABBINIC AUTHORITY

In Jerusalem and the area henceforth called the Land of Israel in Jewish literature, Ezra had brought about a religious reformation of Judaism. He had found a discredited priesthood, failing both in its leadership and religious commitment. He gave them an ultimatum. From now on they could not simply be wealthy aristocrats relying on temple gifts. They had to choose, and only those who took their Jewish religious role seriously would be able to continue in office.

Ezra established a counterbalance to the priesthood. It was a framework for what in time became known as rabbinic authority, a meritocracy made up of scholars. It led directly to a self-perpetuating council based on the biblical idea of the seventy elders whom Moses had assembled to assist him, the Men

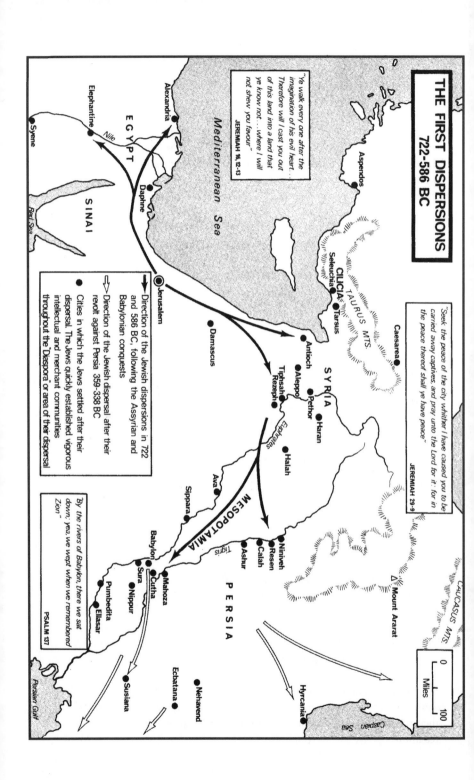

# THE FIRST DISPERSIONS
## 722-586 BC

"Ye walk every one after the imagination of his evil heart... Therefore will I cast you out of this land into a land that ye know not ... where I will not shew you favour."
JEREMIAH 16, 12-13

"Seek the peace of the city whither I have caused you to be carried away captives, and pray unto the Lord for it : for in the peace thereof shall ye have peace"
JEREMIAH 29:9

By the rivers of Babylon, there we sat down, yea, we wept when we remembered Zion."
PSALM 137

Direction of the Jewish dispersions in 722 and 586 BC, following the Assyrian and Babylonian conquests

Direction of the Jewish dispersal after their revolt against Persia 359-338 BC

Cities in which the Jews settled after their dispersal. The Jews quickly established vigorous intellectual and merchant communities throughout the Diaspora or area of their dispersal

Mediterranean Sea

EGYPT

SINAI

Red Sea

Nile

Alexandria
Elephantine
Syene
Daphne

Aspendos

Caesarea

CILICIA
Seleucia
Tarsus
TAURUS MTS.

Jerusalem

Damascus

Antioch

Aleppo
Tiphsah
Rezeph
Pethor
Haran

SYRIA

Euphrates

Halah

Ava

Sippara

MESOPOTAMIA

Babylon
Sura
Mahoza
Cutha
Pumbedita
Nippur
Ellasar

Ashur
Calah
Resen
Niniveh

Tigris

PERSIA

Mount Ararat

CAUCASUS MTS.

Caspian Sea

Hyrcania

Echatana

Nehavend

Susiana

Persian Gulf

0        100
Miles

of the Great Assembly. In due course they would meet in the temple court-yards and became a kind of Supreme Court, later called the *Sanhedrin*. A secondary system was established based on a smaller court called a *Beth Din*, a court of law with a minimum of three judges. Over time the Beth Din would come to be the main structure of Jewish rabbinic authority.

The innovation brought about by Ezra also eventually led to the emergence of two rival sects. They became known as the Sadducees, *Zadokim* in Hebrew after the priestly House of Zadok, and the *Perushim*, the Separatists or Pharisees. The Sadducees were suspicious of Pharisaic interpretations of biblical law because they feared that they might eventually deprive them of their biblical rights and privileges. The Pharisees, on the other hand, felt that the Sadducees' reluctance to be flexible or to accept the Oral Law was simply a way of preserving their status without regard to the needs of the poorer and weaker majority. Despite the impression given by the New Testament, the Pharisees were very much the party of the weaker majority and sympathetic to their needs.

## GREECE AND THE MACCABEANS

Persian power gave way to Greek. In general, the priesthood was more internationally minded and pro-Greek, while the pious rabbinic or Chassidic Jews were poorer, more nationalist and anti-Greek. Such distinctions were not rigid. There were pious priests who sided with the rabbis.

Alexander the Great is said to have passed through the Land of Israel on his way down into Egypt in 332 BCE but to have allowed the Jews to continue their own religious traditions. Legend has it that a meeting took place between the High Priest Simeon the Righteous (Shimon Hatsadik) and Alexander at which, in return for not having his effigy placed in the Temple, all Jewish boys born that year would be named Alexander. He had bigger fish to fry than the small nation perched on the hills around Jerusalem.

After Alexander the Great, the Middle East was torn between the rival claims of the Ptolemies and the Seleucids. Policy towards the Jewish settlement varied from ruler to ruler, but in general the Jews were left alone. Their High Priests became their official representatives to the dominant power, whichever it was, and were soon busy scheming for power. The priesthood became an office that could be bought or acquired through political machinations. So long as the vassal state was submissive, there were no problems. The Seleucids built and maintained a garrison in Jerusalem and the pro-Greek priests willingly brought theatres, circuses and baths into the city.

Jewish nationalism erupted only in response to oppressive rule, as with the Maccabee revolution in 168 BCE. Antiochus IV was impatient (his nickname Epimanes, 'the idiot', as opposed to Epiphanes, 'the Enlightened', gives the game away) and made the mistake of trying to force the Jews to abandon their religion and dedicate their Temple to him. He provoked them into open rebellion.

Judah Maccabee led a guerrilla campaign that succeeded only because of internal divisions in the Syrian capital. He regained control of the Temple, if not the garrison, and rededicated it on the third anniversary of its desecration. The festival of dedication, Chanukah, remains a major Jewish celebration to this day. Despite setbacks, including Judah's death, a Maccabean dynasty was ultimately established under Judah's brother Simon. Slowly, the Maccabeans turned into an aristocracy of their own. They clashed with the Pharisees. Only Queen Salome, the widow of Jannaeus, was sympathetic to rabbinic authority.

The rabbis of the Talmud tried hard to eradicate the Maccabean name and it was only preserved through the Apocryphal Books of the Maccabees that were excluded from the canon. Judah Maccabee is not mentioned in the Talmud. This may be because it was Judah's treaty with Rome that gave the Romans the authority to consider Judea theirs. For this, the rabbis who suffered at Roman hands were not likely to be grateful.

Mainstream Judaism was creative and innovative, though divided. The influence of Greek philosophy and Greek political systems began to exert a major influence on Judaism and even more so on the Jews of the rapidly growing Jewish community in Alexandria, Egypt. Meanwhile, in Babylon, Zoroastrianism and other Eastern traditions had a major impact, acting as a counter-balance to the ideologies of the West and in turn influencing sections of the Judean community.

## ROME

As the Maccabean dynasty declined, so Roman influence began to supersede Greek influence. The Roman preoccupation was more political than ideological. The mainstream Jewish leadership in Jerusalem, the Sadducees, were pro-Roman, whereas the Pharisees were in favour of accommodation. But there were extremist nationalist sects, which wanted to fight the Romans. There were also monastic groups that had withdrawn from the competitive atmosphere of Jerusalem and other cities to retreat to isolation in the Judean wilderness. These groups are known as the Dead Sea sects (although there is still disagreement as to who exactly was whom).

Herod the Idumean defeated the last Hasmonean king, Antigonus, with Roman help and married a Hasmonean princess. He ruled from 37 BCE until 4 CE by exploiting internal Roman politics. After his death, although his son Archelus was nominally in charge, the Romans played a more direct role in running what they saw as their vassal state. After he died, Judea was annexed and procurators put in charge. Political power now was completely in Roman hands.

The turmoil in the Land of Israel about 2,000 years ago was mirrored by tensions in Babylon, Alexandria and Rome. The Alexandrian community in particular was strong and creative. It produced the first significant Jewish philosopher Philo, who lived about the turn of the millennium. Throughout

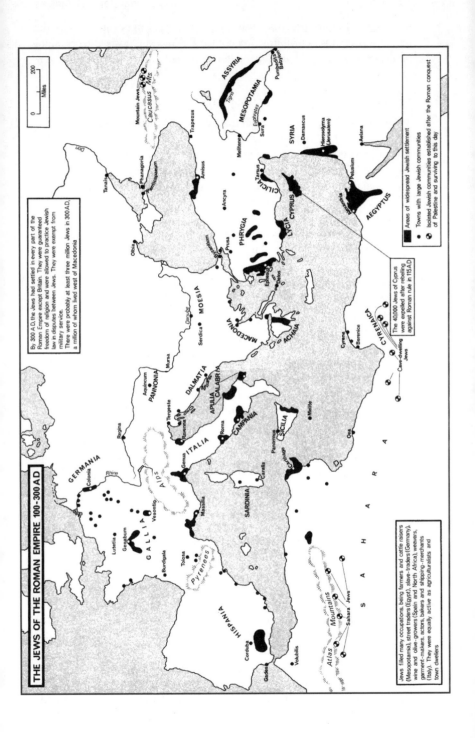

# THE JEWS OF THE ROMAN EMPIRE 100-300 A.D.

By 300 A.D. the Jews had settled in every part of the Roman Empire except Britain. They were guaranteed freedom of religion and were allowed to practice Jewish law in disputes between Jews. They were exempt from military service.

There were probably at least three million Jews in 300 A.D., a million of whom lived west of Macedonia.

Jews filled many occupations, being farmers and cattle raisers (Mesopotamia), street traders (Egypt), slave-traders (Germany), wine and olive-growers (Spain and North Africa), weavers, garment-makers, actors, bakers and shipping-merchants (Italy). They were equally active as agriculturalists and town dwellers.

The 40,000 Jews of Cyprus were expelled after rebelling against Roman rule in 115 A.D.

■ Areas of widespread Jewish settlement

● Towns with large Jewish communities

⊕ Isolated Jewish communities established after the Roman conquest of Palestine and surviving to this day

0 — 200 Miles

the Roman Empire paganism was facing new challenges. In one way this period was creative, religiously. In another, for Judaism, it was the beginning of the process of exile and alienation as a predominantly Diaspora community.

## THE END OF THE SECOND TEMPLE AND EXILE

The policies of the Roman procurators and their insensitivities fanned open rebellion. In 70 CE Vespasian, followed by his son Titus, destroyed Jerusalem and the Second Temple, and hundreds of thousands of Jews were sold into slavery and deported. The main rabbinic party under Yochanan Ben Zakkai was given permission to re-establish its authority in Yavneh by the coast. However it was the north, Galilee, that became the major centre of Jewish life in the Land of Israel.

The rebellions did not end and spread to include Jewish communities around the Roman Empire. The largest of them was in 132 CE when Bar Cochba succeeded in establishing a Jewish State from his headquarters in Bethar, just outside Jerusalem. Many, including the great Rabbi Akiva, believed he was the Messiah precisely because he succeeded in removing foreign domination. It did not last. His death three years later, effectively ended the last hope of Jewish self-rule. It would be 2,000 years before the pendulum would swing back.

After Constantine and his successors, the Land of Israel came under Byzantine control, which proved to be less of a problem than the slow economic decline of the region. Jewish religious authority clung on in a declining state as the other centres increased in power and status.

The Jews now found themselves in two clearly different political worlds, the Roman Empire and the East. For a while Jewish influence in both seemed to be growing and strengthening. In the Roman Empire Jews from the Land of Israel, either as slaves or freemen, began to spread throughout the Roman peninsula and north into Europe. New centres of Jewish life and learning were established in Rome, Bari and Otranto, and from Cyprus to Tunisia. Alexandria became the major centre of Jewish life in the West. Yet tensions between Jews and Greeks were a condition of life in the Diaspora at that time.

## THE BABYLONIAN JEWS

The Babylonian Jewish community had remained powerful ever since its earliest origins. They retained their aristocratic heritage in the form of the Exilarch, who led the communities of the East. During the period of the Second Commonwealth scholars from Babylon had tended to gravitate towards the academies of Israel. Nevertheless, in Babylon their own academies at Nehardea, Machoza, Sura, and Pumbethitha were powerful and effective transmitters of the same rabbinic tradition that Ezra had brought to Israel. The great Hillel had come from Babylon to lead the Jewish academic world from Israel in the first century BCE.

As the Romans degraded Jewish life in Israel, the Babylonian centres grew in stature and power. Ultimately they overtook Israel in importance. The Babylonian Talmud, the great record of Jewish law and lore, was of greater size and significance than the Jerusalem Talmud, and the great Babylonian rabbis took over the baton of religious tradition as the authority of Israel dwindled. The Geonim of Babylon, who succeeded the Talmudic authorities, would become the greatest authority in Judaism until the first millennium CE.

Jews from Babylon began extending their influence eastward and north-east towards Afghanistan and India and into China. They were helped in their Diaspora travels by a common language and patterns of ritual behaviour. Their success was founded on alliances and contacts of family and community that facilitated trade and commerce.

The Persians, who had succeeded the Babylonians and became the major world power to challenge Greece, in general provided a safe haven for the Jews. The Parthians, as they were known, could rely on Jewish support and Jews helped in the campaigns against Greece and Rome. There were periods of Jewish autonomy under the Sassanian dynasties. There were occasional Zoroastrian kings who oppressed the Jews, Jazdegerd II (438–457) and Peroz (457–484), and later Hormizd IV (579–590) who closed the academies. The Jewish tribes of Arabia grew and provided the religious background for the coming Muslim conquest.

The most important satellite community of Babylonia was Kairouan in North Africa. The Geonim of Babylon established satellite academies there and encouraged local leadership entitled the Nagid. It was there that Eldad the Danite appeared in about 900 CE and announced that he had discovered the Ten Lost Tribes living in Africa beyond the river Sambatyon. From Kairouan, Jewish centres spread right along the northern shores of the Mediterranean linking up with the new communities that Islam had allowed to flourish in Spain.

Yemen, too, was a major Jewish centre and did well until the same rampant Islamic spirit of the Almohides found its way there. The new Shiah rulers in the tenth century forced many Jews to convert and we know of their plight from the desperate pleas sent to Maimonides in Cairo and his famous reply on martyrdom in the *Letter to Yemen*. Babylonia would retain important Jewish centres until hostility to the State of Israel in 1948 made life for Jews in many Arab countries untenable.

## UNDER CHRISTIANITY

For a while it looked as though Judaism might even become an accepted religion in the Roman Empire. Its monotheism and involvement in daily life, together with its strong sense of family and education, made it an attractive alternative to paganism. However, its rituals of circumcision, festive days and the Sabbath when no work was allowed, and the restrictions on food presented problems to many that only Christianity's less rigid requirements helped overcome.

To start with, in the fourth century Judaism found itself a recognised religion thanks to Septimius, Caracalla and then the Treaty of Milan in 311. But after Constantine's victories over his rivals, in particular Licinius who was a champion of tolerance, at the Council of Nicaea in 325 Judaism lost its status as a recognised religion in the Roman Empire and found itself struggling against penal laws and limitations. With a brief respite under Julian, Judaism became an outcast religion suffering disadvantages and discrimination. The long night of the Christian Diaspora had begun.

Judaism came to be seen as an 'old', barbaric religion that should now disappear in the face of the new triumphant Christianity. This was reflected in the way the Bible was divided into the Old Testament, supposedly the more primitive early covenant between God and his people, and the New Testament through Jesus that was supposed to have superseded the old. The Old Israel, the Jews, was now replaced by the New Israel, the Church. Yet to this day Jews believe themselves still bound by the original Covenant of Sinai, while Christians have accepted the New Covenant through Jesus and Muslims theirs through Mohammad.

Wherever the Jews moved, from Greece to Spain, throughout the Roman Empire and its successors, they found themselves in ambiguous positions. They played an important role in agricultural, commercial and even political life, and yet they were outsiders and infidels. They were stateless in the sense that identity and community were defined by a religion, Christianity. Their lives and livelihood were entirely dependent on the goodwill of the kings, barons and church leaders in whose realms they found themselves. Sometimes they were encouraged to stay and flourish; on other occasions they were expelled, and more often simply killed. This proved to be true of both the Western and Eastern Christian empires. When they grew tired of fighting amongst themselves or attacking their own heretics, attention turned to the 'stubborn' Jews.

The Code of Theodosius in 379 CE gave some protection to the Jews, while the Council of Toledo in 589 CE imposed very harsh limitations. The Gothic kings, enthusiastic converts to the new order, were not in general friendly to the Jews. It was the Muslim Umayyad invasion of Spain in the eighth century that gave the Jews their one really sympathetic haven on the European mainland.

The migrations during the first millennium took Jews into southern Europe. Italian Jews were in the main the descendents of émigrés from Jerusalem. Although part of the mainstream tradition, they added customs and liturgy unique to themselves. Others moved from the south of France up into England and, by the ninth century, from Metz in France towards Mainz in Germany. This was the path of Rabbeynu Gershon, the Light of the Exile (960–1040), who was accepted as the greatest Jewish authority in Europe of his day.

By the eleventh century Jews had settled in most of the major trading cities of Western Europe and had rabbis of stature and learning. In northern France, Troyes was home to the greatest of commentators and talmudic exegetes, Rabbi Shlomo Yitschaki (1040–1105), known as Rashi, and his descendant Rabbeynu Tam (1080–1171) who dominated Jewish scholarship and still exert a crucial influence. In the south, Provence produced a galaxy of great rabbis and scholars, in particular during the eleventh and twelfth centuries. Major Jewish communities emerged in the Rhineland and areas that we now know as Germany. Another movement spread along the Mediterranean coast into Spain, and a third wave spread through the Balkans and up into the Danube valley.

The north European communities flourished till the Crusades began to spread hatred for the 'enemies of Christ'. Initially, religious zeal led to massacres as enthusiastic crowds, encouraged by evangelical priests, turned on the local aliens in preparation for the campaigns in the Middle East. The Jewish population of York in England was forced into Clifford's Tower and, realising the hopelessness of the situation, took their own lives in 1190.

Popular prejudice was easy to sway in an era of magic, spirits, and superstition. In England a story began to circulate in the twelfth century that Jews needed to kill Christian children and use their blood to make the special bread they ate at Passover or to fill the four cups of wine they drank on Passover Eve. This was ironic. In Christianity the wafer turns into the body of Jesus and the wine into blood. Jews were forbidden to drink blood. When Hugh of Lincoln was found murdered in 1255, Jews were accused of his ritual slaughter. Elsewhere they were found guilty of taking communion wafers to beat the body of Christ until the blood flowed.

It was in Christian Europe too that economic factors also began to play a part. Jews were very often moneylenders and tax farmers because other professions and economic opportunities were closed to them. In places such as Spain, where they had other options in diplomacy, government, commerce and agriculture, they took to them readily.

In many parts of medieval Spain Jews flourished. They were active in literature, science, and medicine. But there, too, they were subject to changes of dynasty and power. Although the 'Golden Age of Spain' produced a magnificent flowering of Jewish literature and scholarship, particularly under Muslim leadership, Jews often suffered changing fortunes and expulsions. Throughout most of England, France, and Germany they were not allowed to join the guilds and only professing Christians could advance.

Although the Fuggers are the fathers of banking, increasingly Jews turned to moneylending and tax farming as a means of survival. Local princelings would use the Jews to raise money and then destroy them as a way of escaping their debts. The Jews found themselves caught between the resentment of those they took taxes from and those above who expected better returns and crueller means of exacting tribute.

The Jews became pariahs both religiously and economically. They were expected to wear distinctive clothes and badges. There were laws forbidding social contact. When economic or social conditions took a turn for the worse Jews were the readily recognisable, universal scapegoats, easy to turn on and to destroy with impunity. This led not only to death but also to expulsion from England in 1292 and slowly from most of Western Europe.

There were sympathetic popes such as Alexander III (1159–1181). But even he, in demanding that Jewish loans to crusaders be cancelled, opened up the way for murder as an easy way of getting the same result. Other popes tried to defend the Jews and reject popular myths, but the power of local demagogues was more effective. In 1298 a Nuremberg nobleman called Rindfleisch accused Jews of pounding a sacred communion wafer until the blood of Jesus flowed and led reprisals, killing the Jews of Rottingen and throughout Franconia, Bavaria and Austria. In the fourteenth century gangs of zealots called the Armleder roved across the same area making similar claims and resulting in equal loss of Jewish life. The Black Death led to charges that the Jews had poisoned the wells, and throughout Europe thousands were massacred.

Rulers, who in the Christian world are fondly remembered, like 'Good King Wenceslaus', German Emperor 1378–1400, were often bad from a Jewish point of view.

## EASTERN EUROPE

In search of refuge the Jews moved eastward into Poland, where for a while they were given a safe haven and encouraged. Boleslav the Pious initially established their rights in 1264 in defiance of Rome. Indeed the bishops and monastic orders constantly agitated against the presence of the Jews. Casimir the Great maintained tolerant policies (1333–1370). But under Vladislav II (1384–1434) persecution began, instigated by the Dominicans. Vladislav also incorporated Lithuania into his empire. This brought suffering to another major Jewish community.

Whereas Casmir IV had welcomed the Jews in 1447, his sons John I in Poland and Alexander in Lithuania both encouraged persecution. The pendulum kept on swinging from encouragement to antagonism. Nevertheless, in Poland Jews achieved a measure of autonomy and freedom that had been denied to them in the West. As a consequence they expanded, and as they did they spread even further eastward towards the Urals in the north and down around the shores of the Black Sea.

In the sixteenth century a Polish government established the *Vaad Arbaa Aratsot* (the Committee of the Four Lands), which in effect governed the Jews of Eastern Europe from the sixteenth until the end of the eighteenth century. It was a council representing Jews from the German borders to Ukraine (Lithuania had its own Vaad). It was oligarchic rather than democratic. Communities sent rabbinic and lay representatives to meet twice yearly at the fairs of Lublin and Yaroslav. It dealt with internal affairs, and fixed commercial and economic conventions. Its laws became the essential tools of adapting Judaism to new situations. The committee was a Supreme Court that the local Jewish courts of law could defer to. It acted as an intermediary between the Crown, the non-Jewish authorities, and the Jews.

The Polish parliament, the Sejm, abolished the council in 1764 and substituted its own poll tax as the means of controlling and dealing with the Jews. Needless to say, this did not endear either party to the other. To Eastern European Jews the Council represented an almost idealistic era of self-governance.

The European Jews developed their own 'private language' called Yiddish, Jewish. It was predominantly a mixture of German and Hebrew, but words were added from the local languages as the Jews moved east. Yiddish was regarded as the vernacular and Hebrew was used only as the sacred language for prayer or scholarship. It also functioned as a cohesive force, but had obvious economic and commercial benefits too. Yet the very factors that helped the Jews retain their identity also marked them out as an alien minority.

As Jews started migrating out of Eastern Europe they tried to acculturate themselves to different languages and cultures. Nevertheless, Orthodoxy retained Yiddish as the preferred language of communication, and the post-Holocaust interest in Eastern European Jewry has led to its survival. The oriental equivalent, Ladino, with Spanish and Arabic at its core, is also experiencing a revival particularly in the field of Music, but it is no longer the day-to-day language of oriental Jews.

## EXPULSION FROM SPAIN 1492

The major expulsion of Jews in the West from Spain in 1492 was followed by expulsions from Portugal, and then the campaigns against those Jews who had converted to Christianity as the lesser of two evils in the hope of surviving death or exile. The Inquisition was primarily directed against these *conversos*, who were accused of diluting true pure Christian blood.

The effect was to push Spanish Jews in two directions. The majority went east, strengthening the Ottoman Empire and establishing centres of Jewish renewal and spirituality in the Galilean hills. The Land of Israel had continued to act as a magnet to Jews in the Diaspora despite hardships, notably during Crusader occupations. After the 1492 expulsions from Spain and Portugal and the ongoing campaigns of the Inquisition, large numbers found their way east and back to their ancestral homeland.

Safed, in the north of the Land of Israel, in particular, became a major centre during the seventeenth century and exercised a profound influence on Jewish life. Joseph Caro (1488–1575) lived there. His legal works became the pivotal texts in popular Jewish Law and are still essential today. The school of Isaac Luria or Arizal (1534–1572), perhaps the greatest of all Kabbalists, had

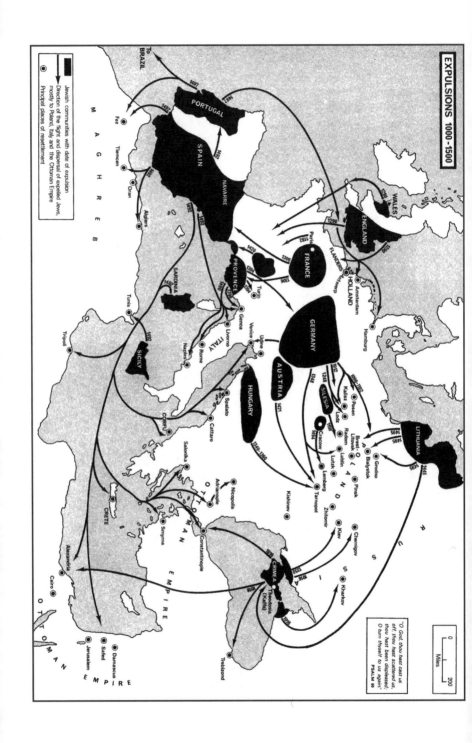

EXPULSIONS 1000-1500

"O God, thou hast cast us
off; thou hast scattered us,
thou hast been displeased;
O turn thyself to us
again."
PSALM 60

Jewish communities with date of expulsion

Direction of the flight and dispersal of expelled Jews,
mostly to Poland, Italy and the Ottoman Empire

Principal places of resettlement

0        200
Miles

a profound influence on Jewish life and customs and was the guiding spirit of the great Chassidic revolution in the eighteenth century.

An influential minority moved north from Iberia to Amsterdam, and thence to London and the New World. These Spanish and Portuguese Jews became known as the Sephardim, the Spanish Jews, as opposed to those of Central and Eastern Europe, who became known as the Ashkenazim. The differences between them were marginal, ritually. But culturally they were very different in the way they perceived themselves and expressed their religious attitudes. Many of those who succeeded in the West soon found it convenient to abandon their Jewish roots.

The first waves of Jewish emigrants westward were in the main financially secure and contributed to the commercial wealth of the new maritime economies they joined. Slowly they began to integrate, even though there were still religious, legal and social barriers to their advancement. Soon poorer immigrants from the east, Ashkenazi Jews, less educated and more conspicuous, joined them. These poorer immigrants were often resented. Nevertheless, they began to add to the complexion of the Jewish communities in Western Europe and the Americas. Together they laid the foundations of the Jewish communities that exist today in the western world.

In Italy Judaism had both flourished and suffered from changing rulers and the varying policies adopted by different popes. In Rome, Jewish scholars were often welcomed. Men like Pico Della Mirandola in the fifteenth century were responsible for a great deal of cultural cross-fertilisation. It was via the influence of Elijah Levita (1469–1549), who taught Sixtus IV, that serious Hebrew study began to spread throughout the Catholic academic world. Johann Reuchlin (1455–1522), who composed a Hebrew grammar and dictionary, became heavily involved in defending Jews and Judaism against the notorious Jewish renegade Pfefferkorn, who allied with the Dominicans in their anti-Jewish campaigns, and Reuchlin suffered greatly as a result.

Meanwhile in the east, the Caliphate welcomed Jews from Zoroastrian oppression. The Jewish communities of Israel persevered in depleted numbers and significance, bypassed by the great Muslim expansion that went on around them. Only during the Crusader kingdoms were Jews completely banished from Jerusalem after the invaders massacred all the non-Christians they could find.

## ISLAM

Although Islam too relegated Jews and Christians to the inferior status of the Dhimmi (the non-Muslim who is not an idol worshipper), and the Pact of Omar in the seventh century had imposed on Jews almost the same restrictions as had Constantine, in general the eastern Jews of Babylon and those of North Africa fared better under Islam than their brothers did under Christianity.

Of course, a great deal depended on who the ruler was and where. The

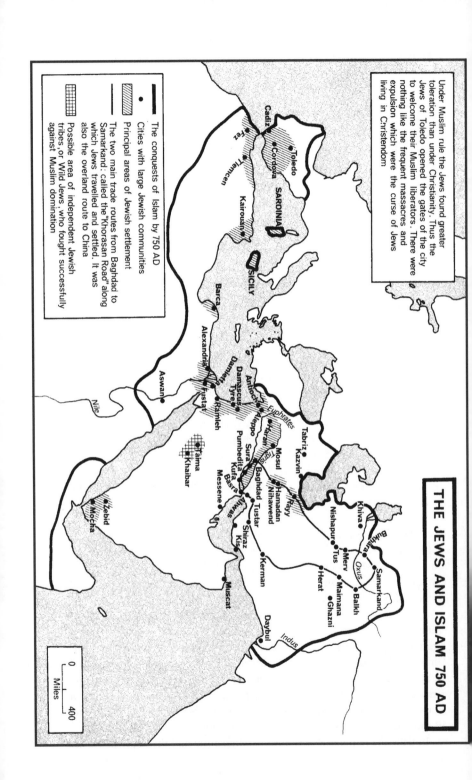

# THE JEWS AND ISLAM 750 AD

Under Muslim rule the Jews found greater toleration than under Christianity. Thus the Jews of Toledo opened the gates of the city to welcome their Muslim liberators. There were nothing like the frequent massacres and expulsion which were the curse of Jews living in Christendom.

- The conquests of Islam by 750 AD
- Cities with large Jewish communities
- Principal areas of Jewish settlement
- The two main trade routes from Baghdad to Samarkand: called the "Khorasan Road" along which Jews travelled and settled. It was also the overland route to China
- Possible area of independent Jewish tribes, or Wild Jews, who fought successfully against Muslim domination

Cadiz, Cordova, Toledo, Fez, Tlemcen, Kairouan, SARDINIA, SICILY, Barca, Alexandria, Aswan, Nile, Fustat, Ramleh, Tyre, Damascus, Antioch, Aleppo, Euphrates, Haran, Tabriz, Kazvin, Mosul, Sura, Pumbedita, Kufa, Baghdad, Basra, Messene, Ahwaz, Tustar, Nihawend, Hamadan, Rayy, Shiraz, Kish, Kerman, Muscat, Daybul, Indus, Khaibar, Taima, Zebid, Mocha, Khiva, Bukhara, Samarkand, Oxus, Maimana, Balkh, Ghazni, Herat, Tus, Merv, Nishapur

0 400 Miles

Umayyad dynasty had created the Golden Age of Spain for the Jews. On the other hand, the Abbasids were initially less well disposed, as were the Fatimids and the Berber dynasties. The Almoravid rulers of Morocco in 1005 insisted on converting the Jews, and the Almohad emperors imposed degrading conditions on Jews living under their more aggressive brand of Islam. Nevertheless, in general, life under Islam was preferable to that under Christianity. The Jews under Islam were the dominant force in Jewry for the first 500 years of Islam. It was only later on, as Islamic power declined in relation to the West, that their influence waned too.

## REFORMATION AND ENLIGHTENMENT

In the sixteenth century two forces exerted new influences on the Jews of Western Europe. The Reformation in the West began to see the modification of Catholic power. Martin Luther initially hoped to win the Jews over to his form of Christianity. In 1523 he wrote, 'Christianity has treated the Jews as though they were dogs not men.' Later on in his life he became embittered by Jewish refusal to join him and expressed very hateful views about 'the Jews and their lies'.

In general, the Protestant schism led to a more amenable climate of opinion towards Jews. Amsterdam, Hamburg, and London in particular emerged as new centres of Jewish life. Menashe Ben Israel, the outstanding leader of Amsterdam Jewry, was invited to England and influenced Cromwell's tolerance of Jewish immigration and the Whitehall Conference of 1655 that debated the issue. The New World opened up new destinations and opportunities. Initially it attracted Jewish refugees from Iberia, but then Central and Eastern European Jews started new waves of emigration.

The Enlightenment also brought about a change in the climate of public opinion, particularly amongst the legislators and the commercial communities. Closing the country to entrepreneurs was seen to have had a negative impact on Iberian commercial life. The emerging economies of Western Europe were all open to new investment, new avenues of capital and a new spirit of enterprise. As a result, Jews began to sense, if not welcome, opportunities for advancement that were closed to them elsewhere. Still, legislative restrictions, limitations on advance in many areas and the religious message of antagonism towards Jews continued to prove the rule.

In Eastern Europe during the Cossack wars, the tension between the Catholics of Poland and the Orthodox Church of the east led to a catastrophic series of massacres in the Chmelniecki campaigns in 1648. The Jews had fought together with the Poles against the Orthodox Cossacks. But sadly in many cases their allies betrayed them. Catholic antagonism to the Jews remained a serious problem. The Cossack campaigns led to a serious decline in the fortunes and mood of Eastern European Jewry. Millions of Jews lived in communities of poverty, alienation and isolation.

Initially the response was to turn to Messianism and the hope that divine intervention would end the agony. The false Messiah Sabbatai Zevi galvanised the whole of European Jewry, from the East to the West, but his failure to materialise as a genuine saviour when he converted to Islam in 1666 led to a collapse of morale. One section of Jewry responded by retreating into an academic and scholastic approach to Judaism. The other adopted the charismatic popularism of the Baal Shem Tov (1700–1776), who founded the Chassidic movement. He combined a popular, neo-kabbalistic form of Jewish practice with an appeal to the simple, uneducated masses. Chassidism was responsible for reviving Jewish life in the East; but it also encouraged a self-sufficiency and sense of alienation from the outside world that resisted the forces of modernism.

In Western Europe Jews tried to integrate into society, but soon discovered that the choice was conversion or continuing discrimination and disadvantage. Jews like Moses Mendelssohn (1729–1786), who translated the Bible into German, began to contribute to Christian society. They were both encouraged and discouraged. Mendelssohn's children felt the need to convert to Christianity in order to progress. Jews were still not allowed to be citizens or enjoy equal rights throughout Europe.

As Napoleonic armies marched eastward through Europe they carried with them an egalitarian approach that swept away the legal restrictions against Jews that had been in place throughout the previous thousand years (much to the disapproval of both the Church and the populace). It is ironic that wherever Napoleon lifted restrictions on the Jews, his enemies reinstated them. Even in England, Jews were not allowed to play a full role in society until the second half of the nineteenth century.

What is more ironic is that the religious leadership of Eastern European Jews was so used to fighting for survival against negative authority that it was worried that the freedoms of liberation would indeed lead to assimilation. Some Chassidic leaders were open in their support of the Tsar against Napoleonic ideology.

## THE PALE OF SETTLEMENT

By the nineteenth century the Jews of Western and Central Europe were flourishing despite their disadvantages. The largest concentration of Jews was in the area that encompassed what are now Poland, Lithuania and Russia, as well as Hungary and Romania. The majority of the Jewish population was concentrated in what, in Russian nineteenth-century terminology, was called the 'Pale of Settlement'. Thus, in 1804 Alexander I decreed that Jews had to live within a designated area that included the 'Thirteen Provinces', five in Lithuania and White Russia, five in the Ukraine, and three in what was Poland. Successive Tsars tried different methods of integrating the Jewish population, sometimes coercive, sometimes educational.

Tsar Nicholas I had thought that by conscripting Jewish children into the army for 25-year periods he could Christianise them. Many thousands perished under the harsh regimes to which they were subjected; others crippled themselves to avoid conscription. This all motivated the massive emigration from Eastern Europe in the nineteenth century.

The Jews of Russia started migrating west, some to Central and Western Europe, but the overwhelming majority went to the *Goldene Medinah* (the United States of America). American Jewry had been established soon after the expulsion from Spain. Its earliest Jewish settlers had come from Sepharadi communities and then from Central Europe. But this new wave helped establish what today is the largest Jewish community outside Israel.

## ZIONISM

Some Jews turned to political activity and helped form revolutionary parties. Others adapted the traditional desire to live in the Holy Land with a new nationalistic ideology and created a new movement they called Zionism. The vast majority were encouraged to stay and retain their closed religious communities and pray and hope for better times. The Zionist movement had many 'midwives' and contributing thinkers, rabbis and activists. It developed into a powerful political force, under the leadership of Theodore Herzl (1860–1904), an assimilated Viennese Jew, who realised that anti-Semitism was not going to go away with modernity. His experience as a journalist at the notorious Dreyfus trial in Paris in 1894 (Dreyfus was a Jewish captain in the French army falsely accused of treason) showed how deep anti-Semitism was, even in a liberated and progressive state. He determined to find Jews a home of their own and he was instrumental in establishing the First Zionist Congress, which met in Basel in 1897.

Zionism's main membership and energy continued to come from Eastern Europe. There, however, Marxism and Socialism drew very heavily on Jewish participation. Many Jews channelled their Messianic hopes into the dream of a new Russia, free and classless. In the struggles Jews were heavily represented on both sides: Bolshevik and Menshevik. Meanwhile, the overwhelming majority of religious Jews steadfastly opposed any attempt to pre-empt the Messianic return to Israel.

The nineteenth century in Europe was a period of massive dislocation. Repressive policies, poverty, and opportunities in the West led to the massive emigration of Jews from the 'Pale of Settlement'. Hundreds of thousands left in successive waves for Western Europe, Argentina and the United States. Some went to the Ottoman Empire, in particular to the Land of Israel.

In eastern societies Jewish communities reflected local conditions; but the one common feature was the gap between the wealthy and the poor. In the nineteenth century the vast majority of Jews throughout the world lived at the lowest levels of society, in spite of the fame of those few Jews like the Rothschilds, who had managed to rise to the very highest echelons of the countries they lived in.

In the nineteenth century Jews began to achieve legal equality just as

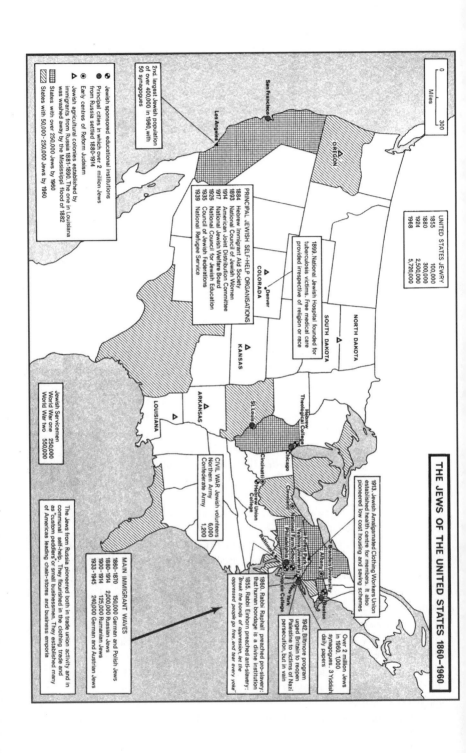

# THE JEWS OF THE UNITED STATES 1860-1960

0 _____ 300
Miles

**UNITED STATES JEWRY**

| 1855 | 100,000 |
| 1880 | 300,000 |
| 1924 | 2,500,000 |
| 1968 | 5,720,000 |

♦ Jewish sponsored educational institutions

● 2nd largest Jewish population of over 400,000 in 1960, with 50 synagogues

● Principal cities in which over 2 million Jews from Russia settled 1880-1914

◉ Early centres of Reform Judaism

▲ Jewish agricultural colonies established by immigrants from Russia 1881-1890. The one in Louisiana was washed away by the Mississippi flood of 1882

░ States with over 250,000 immigrants from Russia 1881-1914

▨ States with 50,000-250,000 Jews by 1960

1899. National Jewish Hospital founded for tuberculosis victims. Free medical care provided irrespective of religion or race

**PRINCIPAL JEWISH SELF-HELP ORGANISATIONS**
1884 Hebrew Immigrant Aid Society
1893 National Council of Jewish Women
1914 American Joint Distribution Committee
1917 National Jewish Welfare Board
1926 National Council for Jewish Education
1935 Council of Jewish Federations
1939 National Refugee Service

1913. Jewish Amalgamated Clothing Workers Union established health centre for members. It also pioneered low cost housing and saving schemes

Over 2 million Jews in 1960, 1000 synagogues, 3 Yiddish daily papers

1942. Biltmore program urged Britain to reopen Palestine to victims of Nazi persecution, but in vain

1860. Rabbi Raphall preached pro-slavery; that human bondage is a divine institution
1855. Rabbi Einhorn preached anti-slavery: 'Break the bonds of oppression, let the oppressed people go free and tear every yoke'

**CIVIL WAR** Jewish volunteers
Northern Army 6,000
Confederate Army 1,200

**MAIN IMMIGRANT WAVES**

| 1860-1870 | 150,000 German and Polish Jews |
| 1880-1914 | 2,000,000 Russian Jews |
| 1900-1914 | 125,000 Rumanian Jews |
| 1933-1945 | 240,000 German and Austrian Jews |

Jewish Servicemen
World War one 250,000
World War two 550,000

The Jews from Russia pioneered both in trade union activity and in communal self-help. They flourished in the clothing trade and as 'custom peddlers' or small businessmen. They established many of Americas leading chain-stores and business emporia

OREGON
COLORADO · Denver
SOUTH DAKOTA
NORTH DAKOTA
KANSAS
ARKANSAS
LOUISIANA
San Francisco
Los Angeles
St. Louis
Chicago
Cincinnati · Hebrew Union College
Cleveland
Baltimore
Hebrew Theological College
National Farm School · Philadelphia
Dropsie College
Forest Park · New York
Brandeis University · Boston
Albany
Yeshiva University

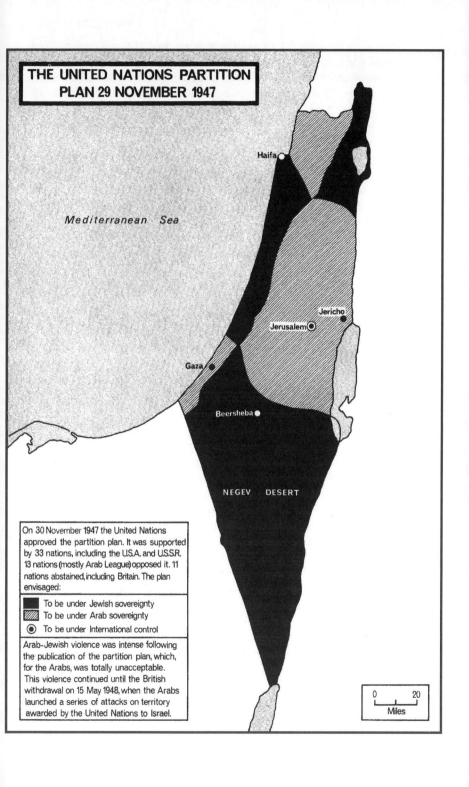

# THE UNITED NATIONS PARTITION PLAN 29 NOVEMBER 1947

Haifa○

*Mediterranean Sea*

Jericho●

Jerusalem◉

Gaza●

Beersheba●

NEGEV DESERT

On 30 November 1947 the United Nations approved the partition plan. It was supported by 33 nations, including the U.S.A. and U.S.S.R. 13 nations (mostly Arab League) opposed it. 11 nations abstained, including Britain. The plan envisaged:

◼ To be under Jewish sovereignty
▨ To be under Arab sovereignty
◉ To be under International control

Arab-Jewish violence was intense following the publication of the partition plan, which, for the Arabs, was totally unacceptable. This violence continued until the British withdrawal on 15 May 1948, when the Arabs launched a series of attacks on territory awarded by the United Nations to Israel.

0          20
Miles

nationalism became the movement that replaced the old Empires. New pseudo-scientific ideas of true, pure nations and races began to create a climate of anti-Semitism based less on religion and more on racial grounds. Jews were free to live in western countries but were made to feel different and even unwanted, no matter how great their contribution to art, music, literature, and commerce. Not even excessive patriotism would save them from racist antagonism.

By the end of the nineteenth century, the Jewish communities of Western Europe and the New World were already beginning to move the centre of gravity of Jewish life. Religious centres in Eastern Europe and in Jerusalem were still the dominant spiritual influences. The twentieth century began with anti-Semitic outrages. The Kishinev massacres in 1903 were the worst. They appear to have been instigated by Russian governmental sources, which were also held responsible for the notorious forgery *The Protocols of the Elders of Zion*, purporting to be evidence of a Jewish plot to master the world. It can still be found on anti-Semitic bookshelves. The massacres were followed by the last blood-libel in Russia at which a Jew was accused of killing a Christian child for its blood during the Beilis Trial (1911–1913). It is hardly surprising that so many Jews welcomed the possibility of a revolution. Yet Jews found themselves fighting each other in the armies of all the world powers during the Great War.

## THE BALFOUR DECLARATION AND ISRAEL

The First World War brought about the first of three crucial and radical changes in Jewish life. Allenby's capture of Jerusalem and the collapse of the Ottoman Empire led to the Balfour Declaration of 1917, allowing for the possibility of a Jewish homeland in what had come to be called Palestine. The Zionist movement had been encouraging immigration since the end of the nineteenth century. In the main these new pioneers were left-wing, socialist and secular, a new breed of Jew from the traditional Orthodox Jews who had come to the Land of Israel not to rebuild it but rather to keep the old flames of tradition alive. The tensions that developed between the pioneers and the Arabs, as well as with the traditional Jews of the old settlements, would colour Jewish life throughout the coming century.

The Balfour Declaration was a statement of policy made in a private letter from Arthur Balfour, then British Secretary of State for Foreign Affairs, to Lord Rothschild. It said that the Government viewed with approval the idea of a Jewish homeland in the Land of Israel. Previous offers of a Jewish homeland in Uganda had been voted down at the Zionist Congress of 1904. Most of the more assimilated Jews of Britain and America were against the declaration. They saw themselves as Americans or Englishmen first and Jews second. They feared that a Jewish State would increase anti-Semitism by laying Jews open to charges of dual loyalties. Over time such opposition disappeared, particularly in the light of Nazism.

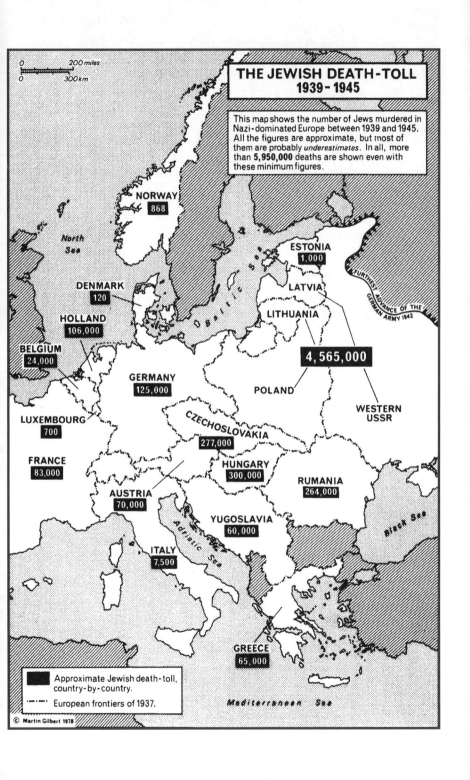

# THE JEWISH DEATH-TOLL 1939-1945

This map shows the number of Jews murdered in Nazi-dominated Europe between 1939 and 1945. All the figures are approximate, but most of them are probably *underestimates*. In all, more than **5,950,000** deaths are shown even with these minimum figures.

0   200 miles
0   300 km

*North Sea*

NORWAY
868

ESTONIA
1,000

LATVIA

DENMARK
120

LITHUANIA

HOLLAND
106,000

*Baltic Sea*

FURTHEST ADVANCE OF THE GERMAN ARMY 1942

BELGIUM
24,000

GERMANY
125,000

4,565,000

POLAND

WESTERN USSR

LUXEMBOURG
700

CZECHOSLOVAKIA
277,000

FRANCE
83,000

HUNGARY
300,000

AUSTRIA
70,000

RUMANIA
264,000

*Adriatic Sea*

YUGOSLAVIA
60,000

*Black Sea*

ITALY
7,500

GREECE
65,000

■ Approximate Jewish death-toll, country-by-country.
—·—·— European frontiers of 1937.

© Martin Gilbert 1978

*Mediterranean Sea*

The Russian Revolution effectively put an end to Jewish religious creativity in the Soviet Union and the Nazi Holocaust effectively destroyed the religious and secular Jewish communities of Central and Eastern Europe. Out of these disasters two new centres emerged, America and Israel.

Many of the earliest Zionist pioneers had dreamed of a multinational secular state in which Jews and Arabs would coexist. Indeed many of the European academics who escaped from Nazism and came to live there, such as Martin Buber and Gershom Scholem, advocated this throughout their lives. Israel formally accepted the United Nations partition plan in 1947. Sadly, Arab nationalism rejected partition. In 1948 Israel declared independence and was recognized by the United Nations. The result has been continuing conflict between Israeli and Arab that has had a detrimental impact on both societies.

Although there are Jewish centres outside Israel, primarily America, France and the United Kingdom, and other lesser communities throughout the free world, such as South Africa and Australia, there are now no Jewish communities of any significance surviving in the Arab world, except for Morocco. Those North African Jews who did not emigrate to Israel moved to France.

Since its establishment as a Jewish home, Israel's academic and religious institutions have overtaken those of every other Jewish centre in expertise and influence. The mass immigration of Jews from Arab lands helped create the first truly international and multicultural Jewish centre for 2,000 years.

## THE HOLOCAUST

The destruction by the Nazis of more than 6 million Jews was the culmination of 2,000 years of European anti-Semitism. No single factor can explain the continuing hatred. Part is due to Christianity's teaching of contempt. Modern Nationalism together with racial theories propounded by 'scientists' also played a prominent part. Anti-Semitism has been endemic in Europe for so long that the debate regarding its causes continues.

The effect this has had on Jews has been profound and far-reaching. The feeling that the world stood by and did nothing has emphasised Jewish feelings of alienation and isolation, and the reaction of the world powers afterwards certainly helped towards the establishment of a Jewish State.

For many years the Holocaust was largely suppressed as a subject for psychological reasons, but the more recent outpouring of history, literature, and art have turned it into an alternative icon of Jewish identity. The religious world sees the Holocaust as just the culmination of the agony of the Exile; the secular world sees it as a unique horror.

After Israel, the Holocaust has been the major factor in reshaping Jewish communities and affecting the psyche and self-perception of Jews today. These influences will be explored in greater detail in the chapters on theology and Judaism today.

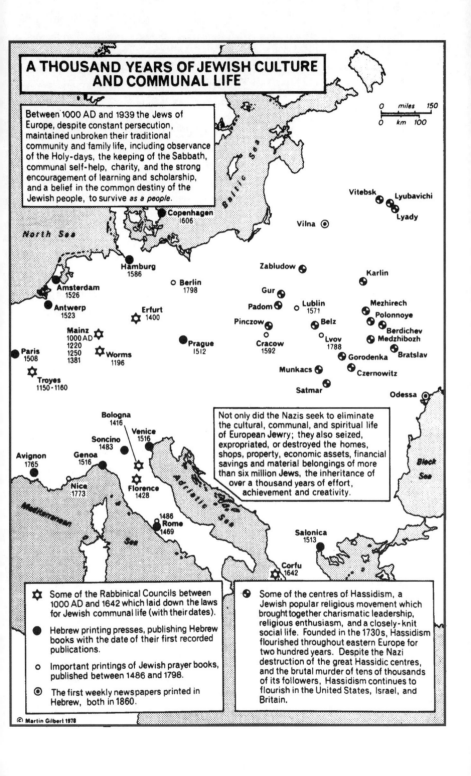

# A THOUSAND YEARS OF JEWISH CULTURE AND COMMUNAL LIFE

Between 1000 AD and 1939 the Jews of Europe, despite constant persecution, maintained unbroken their traditional community and family life, including observance of the Holy-days, the keeping of the Sabbath, communal self-help, charity, and the strong encouragement of learning and scholarship, and a belief in the common destiny of the Jewish people, to survive *as a people*.

O miles 150
O km 100

Vitebsk ✦ Lyubavichi
Lyady

Copenhagen
1606

Vilna ⊙

North Sea

Zabludow ✦

Karlin ✦

Hamburg
1586

O Berlin
1798

Gur ✦
Padom ✦
Pinczow ✦

Lublin
O 1571

Mezhirech ✦
Polonnoye ✦
Berdichev ✦
Medzhibozh ✦

Amsterdam
1526

Antwerp
1523

Erfurt
1400 ✡

Mainz ✡
1000 AD
1220
1250
1381

Prague
1512

Belz ✦

Cracow
1592

O Lvov
1788

Paris
1508

Worms ✡
1196

Troyes
1150-1160 ✡

Munkacs ✦

Gorodenka ✦
Bratslav ✦

Czernowitz ✦

Satmar ✦

Odessa ⊙

Bologna
1416

Venice
1516

Not only did the Nazis seek to eliminate the cultural, communal, and spiritual life of European Jewry; they also seized, expropriated, or destroyed the homes, shops, property, economic assets, financial savings and material belongings of more than six million Jews, the inheritance of over a thousand years of effort, achievement and creativity.

Soncino
1483

Avignon
1765

Genoa
1516

Nice
1773

Florence
1428 ✡

Adriatic Sea

Black Sea

Mediterranean Sea

1486
Rome
1469

Salonica
1513

Corfu
1642 ✡

© Martin Gilbert 1978

✡   Some of the Rabbinical Councils between 1000 AD and 1642 which laid down the laws for Jewish communal life (with their dates).

●   Hebrew printing presses, publishing Hebrew books with the date of their first recorded publications.

○   Important printings of Jewish prayer books, published between 1486 and 1798.

⊙   The first weekly newspapers printed in Hebrew, both in 1860.

✦   Some of the centres of Hassidism, a Jewish popular religious movement which brought together charismatic leadership, religious enthusiasm, and a closely-knit social life. Founded in the 1730s, Hassidism flourished throughout eastern Europe for two hundred years. Despite the Nazi destruction of the great Hassidic centres, and the brutal murder of tens of thousands of its followers, Hassidism continues to flourish in the United States, Israel, and Britain.

# Chapter 2

# A Theological Overview: 1

## THE BEGINNINGS (2000 BCE–1300 BCE)

About 4,000 years ago religions were an essential and all-embracing way of life, not just one aspect of it. They were associated with and underpinned authority and identity. They sought to address basic human questions and insecurities and bring order to life.

### The Biblical Narrative

Early Judaism is often called biblical Judaism, although traditional Jews would not accept the implications that biblical and later Judaism are distinct. The Bible charts the evolution of the human encounter with God. Adam and Eve, childlike, were reactive to instructions and God appeared as the formidable and frightening parent, giving rules and punishing. The biblical texts have been interpreted in so many different ways by so many different traditions. Judaism has its own way of looking at its religious sources. Often there are contradictory traditions of interpretation, but certain themes have become dominant.

As an example, most readings of the biblical text did not see the error of Adam and Eve as 'original sin' but as a symptom of the failure of humans to follow God and, as humans, being inclined to make mistakes. It is as though God desperately wanted humans to function effectively and ethically without needing to intervene. Repeated failures led to the flood and later to a more detailed revelation of the divine framework for living.

Cain and Abel introduced the idea of sacrifices. Cain expected a straightforward response as one might expect from a human. He could not understand God's message that one might need to persevere to attain a genuine closeness to the Divine. He failed to make the connection between God and ethical behaviour.

The line of Cain came to an end after seven generations. Meanwhile Adam had started again. His grandson Enosh was 'called in the name of God'. This initiated the process of verbal communication with God, prayer. A few generations on, Chanoch (called Enoch in the translation; there are two, one in the Cain line, but here we are speaking about the Adam line) 'walked with God' but was taken away. Following the theme of religious evolution, Chanoch thought that walking with God implied that one ought to withdraw from society rather than stay within it and try to change it.

These were all stages in the process of exploring the divine-human relationship. Yet none of them, even Noah, was regarded as the 'finder of truth' or had an impact on a corrupt society. Noah failed to get anyone beyond his family to join him.

It is Abram who is regarded as the first monotheist, the founder of the Jewish tradition. According to biblical tradition, Abram's family emigrated from the Tigris-Euphrates basin up to Haran in the north. After Abram's father died there, Abram journeyed south with his wife Sarai and his nephew Lot and entered the land of Canaan. There he was free to offer up sacrifices to the One God.

Abram is characterised as someone who cared for others. Despite Sodom's immorality Abram argued with God and desperately tried to save the city from destruction: 'Will the Judge of all the earth not be just?' (Genesis 18.25). He interacted with a range of different personalities and tribes. In Canaan Abram encountered good people as well as bad. Melchizedek, a priest to El Elyon (another name for the God of Abram), offered him hospitality and tithes. He made treaties and pacts with the various kingdoms around him, notably with Abimelech King of Gerar, and later with Ephron the Hittite.

Despite God's promises, Abram had to fight for virtually every aspect of his life. Having a close relationship with God did not guarantee an easy time. No wonder some rabbis saw a connection between Abram and Job, the suffering servant of God. The relationship with God transformed Abram and his name was changed to Abraham and Sarai's to Sarah. The extra letter in both names is the letter hay, the Hebrew symbol for God, the added dimension. The bond between Abraham and God is sealed through the first commandment of the Bible, male circumcision (Genesis 17).

Finally, Abram got his son through Sarah, Isaac. The story of his near sacrifice (Genesis 22) has become emblematic. In Judaism its significance lies in the extent to which worship of God has certain boundaries and limitations.

This relationship with God was sustained through the more passive character of Isaac, who followed less flamboyantly in his father's footsteps, and on through Jacob. Jacob was in a constant state of conflict, with his brother Esau, then his father-in-law Laban and finally with his own children. After Jacob fought the angel (Genesis 32), his name was changed to Israel, which literally translated means 'he who fights with man and God and succeeds'. The implication was that a spiritual life would involve constant struggle, both with man and God. The relationship with God would be one of engagement rather than passive acceptance.

Ritual begins to play a part in the way human beings interact with God. From the story of Noah we have learnt that there were 'pure' animals that could be sacrificed and 'impure' ones that could not. The early biblical law commemorated the fight between Jacob and the angel by forbidding his descendents to eat the sinew that runs through the thigh joint. The whole system of integrating social and moral standards with rituals was slowly developing.

Rivalries and tensions, Isaac and Yishmael, Jacob and Esau, and Joseph and his brothers, ran right through the biblical narrative. There were no saints, no perfect human beings. Life was a constant challenge. It was the experience of Egyptian slavery that became the crucible out of which a new religion emerged.

After the early failure of mankind to live without an imposed religious system, the vehicle that God used for this new approach in giving guidance to mankind was the Children of Israel. Despite being 'selected' to become the example of how to live a godly life, the biblical narrative consistently described the limitations if not the errors both of the founding fathers Abraham, Isaac and Jacob, and also of the people of Israel. Their 'election' was not a matter of conveying superiority but rather obligation. It would be the Torah, the general term that applies both to the Five Books of Moses and the general corpus of Jewish Law, custom and interpretation, which would offer a system of integrating morality with behavioural rituals.

Was this role of Israel a temporary one? Judaism has always insisted that it remains committed to the original covenant. Certainly Jews would accept that they have not always lived up to their mission. Nevertheless, they would argue that the mission itself and the content of the Sinai revelation remain as relevant today as then. Some would say that by 'giving birth' to Christianity and Islam, Judaism inspired more popular versions, adapted for a wider audience.

## Biblical Law

To Jews the essence of biblical law remains a powerful relevant guide. It has been suggested that there was no distinction in the Bible between ritual, civil and ethical laws. In principle this is right. God was and is the sole authority upon which the whole system is built and obedience to divine authority as opposed to human deduction is the primary motive for Jewish behaviour (one of Kant's objections to Judaism). Nevertheless, the Torah itself drew the distinction between 'Commands, Ritual Laws and Civil Laws' (Deuteronomy 1 and 6).

The Torah created a complex national system of behaviour and worship built around its society, the tabernacle and the priesthood. There was a balance between the communal and the individual, and between public worship on the one hand and the home and private obligation on the other.

The majority of the biblical legal system was devoted to the role of the priest, the sacrificial system, its allied purity laws and the tabernacle (which was later superseded by the Temple). In terms of ritual, the emphasis was on the public ceremonial. However, there are three clear categories of law that extended beyond the tabernacle.

*Civil Law*

The civil laws, described by the Hebrew word *mishpatim*, covered the whole areas of commercial and social interaction in society. Laws given in Exodus, Leviticus and Deuteronomy concerned agriculture, commerce, property transfers, guardianship, damages, currency, employment practice and slavery, both internal and external, charity, social obligations and laws of marriage, divorce and inheritance. Underlying these laws was the legal system as an objective standard, offering everyone recourse to law.

The notion of 'justice' and 'righteousness' was a repeated theme, as was the importance of an honest and independent judiciary. There needed to be at least three judges and the majority decided. But this system was neither rigidly legalistic, devoid of humanity, nor inflexible. The commonly quoted biblical phrase 'an eye for an eye and a tooth for a tooth' (Exodus 21 and Leviticus 24) was surrounded each time it appeared in the text by laws that demanded financial rather than literal compensation. Shylock's pound of flesh would have made no sense to biblical legislators. A sitting judge would have needed some guidance when faced with a toothless man who had knocked out the tooth of a normally dentured compatriot. The Oral Law was the supplementary mechanism that explained how biblical laws were carried out in practice.

One of the remarkable features of the biblical legal system was the degree to which women were treated equally in the civil sense. Of course, society was essentially patriarchal. But biblical civil law did not differentiate between the sexes on issues of life and death or damages, and insisted that women had marital rights and enforceable protection. Rape was equated with murder (Deuteronomy 22.26), and even in matters of tribal inheritance women could inherit in the absence of sons. Women were however excluded from the judicial system.

A cursory look at biblical law leaves us with the impression that the death penalty was the most common method of civil control. In fact the biblical system required two witnesses before a conviction could be achieved. There was no room for circumstantial evidence, the basis of most of our criminal convictions today. Thus, it was not easy to convict. If one adds the require-ment of 'warning', understood as the need for two independent witnesses to affirm that the perpetrator was warned both of the crime and of the punish-ment that went with it, then one is bound to wonder what the purpose of the repeated death penalty was. It is likely that it played a role in underscoring the relative importance of different actions. It is often through the punish-ment prescribed that one can establish the degree to which a society values certain actions over others. The number of times death was prescribed for offences against parents combines with the command to respect and love in such a way as to underline the essential role of family in the biblical mindset.

Chapters 21 to 24 of Exodus presented the initial phase of the civil programme. They covered issues of damages to property and person, drawing a distinction between murder and manslaughter. They called for perpetrators of violence to be responsible for paying for loss of employment, as well as medical expenses, and included rules protecting slaves, guaranteeing certain basic 'rights', and regulating the conditions and rules for compensating people injured by animals. Similarly, there were rules designed to protect animals and that required individuals to help in situations where humans or animals were suffering. There was defined responsibility for causing damage both directly and indirectly.

Obligations were laid down for a person who borrowed or was given charge of someone else's property or livestock. There were rules governing theft, and rules governing lending money or objects. Yet every time the Bible gave a list of these civil laws others were intertwined relating to charity and treatment of the poor, as well as what we would call ritual laws.

As time wore on, the expansion of Jewish law continued and indeed continues as it met and meets new circumstances. But the biblical laws remained the basic foundation on which later legislation was built.

### Ethics

The second area of biblical concern is what we might call the ethical, described by the general Hebrew term *mitzvah*, command, and sometimes the multifunctional word Torah. The well-known 'Love your neighbour as yourself' is often mistakenly attributed to the New Testament. Its source is Leviticus chapter 19 where other ethical commands included not hating one's neighbour, not putting a stumbling block before the blind or cursing the deaf, and rebuking an offender so that he realises what is wrong. These were combined with the almost ubiquitous exhortation to remember what it was like to be a slave, repeated more than any other phrase in the Bible, and the command to look after the widow and the orphan, the second most repeated phrase. The concern for welfare extended beyond the Children of Israel themselves to include 'the stranger dwelling in your midst'. The charity laws were extensive and were expressed through the main industry of the time, agriculture. We can see from the Book of Ruth how the commands allowing the poor to glean were open to aliens as well. Underlying the charity rules was the requirement to help the indigent re-establish themselves. Debtors could become Hebrew slaves to work off their obligations. As Hebrew slaves they retained full civil rights and obligations and on release they had to be provided with sufficient means to avoid returning to dependence. Lending money came under the charity laws rather than the commercial, in that charging interest was forbidden so as to enable the poor to borrow without serious penalty.

### Ritual Law

The idea of the *chok*, the law that has no utilitarian function, explains what we would call ritual law. This term covered perhaps the largest number of laws in the Bible. The sacrificial system and its allied area of ritual purity occupied more than half of the corpus of biblical legislation and, after the destruction of the Second Temple 2,000 years ago, it became of academic interest (although there are Jews who study these laws in the hope that the Temple will be rebuilt). But under the heading of chok came the dietary laws and the festivals, as well as the Seventh Day, Shabbat, an essential element in the biblical system.

The category of chok also included the sexual laws, both those limiting whom one could marry and those regulating behaviour with one's own wife. There was no biblical word for incest, just the general word *ervah* (nakedness, sexual immorality), which characterised all forbidden unions in the Bible.

The idea of chok was that it was an act of obedience to divine authority that had no obvious utilitarian motive. Although it is common now to try and find reasons for such questions as why some animals were forbidden, the Bible gave nothing away. Rarely, as in the case of the laws limiting the role of the king so that money and women should not distract him from him responsibilities, did the Bible give reasons for its prohibitions. In general, the Torah expected obedience as an acceptance of superior divine authority. Only indirectly could one deduce the consequences, a just and equitable society.

## The Image of God

It is often suggested that the God of the Old Testament was an angry vengeful God concerned only with punishment and law. Objective scrutiny does not bear this out. The image conveyed is indeed of a powerful force, master of the universe, but also a parental one, caring, giving direction and correction. The theme of forgiveness features all the time in the Bible from Cain onwards as the Children of Israel consistently rebelled against divine authority. The command to love God was repeated much more often than the command to 'fear', and the word that is translated as 'fear' would be more appropriately translated as 'respect'. Identical terms were used to describe the relationship between children and parents and that between humans and God.

The other 'theological' feature of the Bible is that there was no law that commanded belief. The first of the so-called Ten Commandments was formulated 'I am the Lord your God', rather than 'You must believe I am the Lord your God'. On the other hand, later on, the Bible commands 'to love the Lord your God'. This was the phrase that became part of the *Shema*, the most important confession of a Jew. Abstract belief was mentioned only once and that was with regard to Abraham's relationship with God. Even then, the word *emunah*, often translated as 'belief', better translates as firmness of resolve. The word was used to convey reliability rather than theological conviction.

The God of the Bible was one who had to be encountered and experienced rather than understood abstractly. When Moses asked God at the burning bush (Exodus 3.13) for his name, he received a rather puzzling response. However one translates the Hebrew reply 'I Am what I Am' (Exodus 3.13), the answer was not a rational one. It is true that the Hebrew word YHVH is a combination of the Hebrew words for past, present and future. In theory this could mean that God was and is above and beyond time. But one is bound to wonder whether that would have been the message the toiling Hebrew slaves would have responded to. An alternative understanding is that this is an assertion about God in history. But this too seems anachronistic. Neither of them tells us about God, but rather about his impact on humanity. Similarly, the later response that 'no man can see Me and live' (Exodus 33.20) was not a philosophical statement. God was simply beyond human comprehension, in contrast to other pagan gods.

Another impediment to understanding the biblical notion of God is the fact that in biblical Hebrew there are seven distinct words for God, whereas in English there is only one. El (with a root meaning up), Elohim (a word also used to mean 'Judges'), Shaddai (Head of Spirits), Tsevaot (meaning Hosts, incorporating all the other forces of the universe) Adonai (Master), Yah and YHVH (the construct of the words for present, past and future, a sort of non-visual transcendent force). The biblical tradition accepted that God had different 'faces', appearing to humans in different manifestations, but remained a force that was and is non-material and not to be represented in any way.

## Public Worship

Important as the biblical emphasis on the tabernacle was, in practice biblical life functioned on two levels. There were the public community sacrifices and rituals that the priests carried out on behalf of everyone else. But equally important were those rituals for individuals, centred more on the home than on the public arena.

After the well-organised and centrally controlled life in the desert, the tabernacle became more remote from most of the tribes. Even when the Temple was constructed in Jerusalem the average person would only visit occasionally. The actual way festivals were celebrated by the priests differed radically from the way in which the average citizen celebrated them. In effect there were two parallel systems, one followed by the priesthood in the Temple and the other followed by the masses.

## Eschatology

The biblical texts made no direct mention of concepts such as the afterlife or resurrection. This is surprising given that all the surrounding tribes had rather sophisticated systems for dealing with death and preparing bodies to face the next phase of their journey. One need only think of Egypt with its mummies and pyramids. Was this a conscious attempt to present an opposing view of life and death with the emphasis on this world now? Or was it that the Torah was simply more concerned with the more universal and immediate areas of behaviour? Perhaps it was a positive idea about the continuity of life, of the unity of matter and spirit.

## Religion in the Promised Land

After the death of Moses and the invasion of Canaan the tribes lost their cohesion. They abandoned their tradition for those of the pagan tribes around them. The attraction of paganism lay in its sexual freedom and temple prostitution. The earlier success of the Midianites in seducing the people, as described in the Book of Numbers, hinted at the Achilles heel of the Hebrew tribes. Their tradition was perceived as one of restraint. Paganism offered the opposite.

The Bible in Deuteronomy laid down a series of contradictory models for leadership. On the one hand, grudging acceptance of a king was hemmed in with limitations and a clear exhortation that the Torah should exercise constraint over his power. Against the king was set the role of the priest, as well as those of the judge and the prophet. Exactly what the division of labour between them was initially was not made clear, but over the next 200 years or so a pattern began to emerge.

## THE FIRST SETTLEMENT (1300 BCE–586 BCE)

Moses was succeeded by Joshua who exercised unchallenged authority. After him, no one achieved similar acceptance until Samuel, several hundred years later. The Judges, men and women, achieved prominence on the basis of their own qualities and their ability to re-energise the tribes and bring them back to some form of loyalty to their own traditions.

Tribal divisions were maintained and divisiveness increased. After the famous case of the concubine in Gibeah (Judges 19), there was all-out war between Benjamin and the other tribes that nearly led to the extinction of Benjamin. During this period the priesthood seemed to have failed in most of its functions. It is only with the last of the Judges, Samuel, that the roles of priest and the judge were combined in one person for the first time, successfully. But it did not last and towards the end of his life Samuel was constrained to appoint a king.

## Prophets

It is at this stage that we hear of the schools of the Prophets for the first time. The term navi (prophet) was used both of Abraham and Miriam, but it was now applied to those who kept the religious flame alive amongst the populace. Schools of prophets toured the country, bands of young enthusiasts, singing and indulging in ecstatic fits of worship. They offered an alternative camaraderie to the usual activities of agricultural labour or war.

The king together with the priests represented an aristocratic hierarchy that controlled the tools of state and formal religion. The prophet, on the other hand, emerged as the charismatic individualist. He or she had no official position, but was able to bring a message of moral authority or spiritual strength to the people from which he or she sprung.

Where leadership was appointed, men preserved these positions for themselves. However, in spheres that relied on personal charisma and personal qualities women featured and were able to achieve the highest positions. Excluded from the monarchy and priesthood, there were women judges and prophets.

The tension between king and prophet continued throughout the period of the first kingdom. It started with the prophet Nathan's objection to David's behaviour over Bathsheba (2 Samuel 12). His wonderful parable of the rich man stealing the poor man's only sheep was impressive both in its language and in the fact that he dared to face the omnipotent king with his condemnation. Equally impressive was the king's willingness to be excoriated in this way. This fearless moral authority continued with the struggle of Elijah and Elisha against Ahab and Jezebel of the northern kingdom. It was sustained despite pressure, and such spiritual giants as Jeremiah were imprisoned for castigating the Judean leadership over its Babylonian policy.

The prophets did not appear to be religious innovators. Much is made of their criticism of the hypocrisies of the Temple system, but it makes no sense to regard them as reformers. On the contrary, they wanted to reinforce the tradition and return to its purity of intent and ideal. If they criticised the abuse of the system, it was specifically the abuses that they railed against. There were very rare instances of prophetic innovation.

### The First Schism

The united kingdom of the twelve tribes lasted until Solomon's successor Rehoboam. Then the tribes split into two camps, barely 500 years after the Exodus. Judah and Benjamin stayed loyal to the House of David and maintained their presence around Jerusalem and to the south. The other ten tribes set up a northern state around the cities of Bethel and Dan.

The northern kingdom was faced with a major religious issue. The biblical tradition of pilgrim festivals required every male to go up to Jerusalem three times a year, at Passover, Pentecost and Tabernacles, to appear in the Temple. One of the obligatory biblical tithes, maaser sheni, had to be set aside to be eaten or its monetary value taken to buy food in Jerusalem on the three annual pilgrim festivals. No new kingdom could sanction its citizens going to another rival country and contributing to its economy regularly each year.

So competing temples were built in Dan and Bethel. In them were placed two golden calves. The northern tribes transferred their religious loyalty to these two new sanctuaries. This illustrates the extent to which the golden calf remained a central cult amongst many of the tribes. It also underlines the extent to which the north had its own alternative religious structure.

When the northern kingdom was finally destroyed by Sargon in 722 BCE, the ten tribes were replaced with other peoples from the Assyrian empire. They came to be known as the Samaritans, named after Samaria, the capital of the north that King Omri built. They were influenced by the religions of both the north and the south. On the one hand, they remained loyal to the biblical text and traditions of the south, but they established their own sanctuary on Mount Gerizim. In fact Mounts Gerizim and Eyval were mentioned in Deuteronomy, whereas Jerusalem was not. So they had some justification in their deviation. But there was no evidence that they built or worshipped golden calves.

### The Babylonian Exile

In Babylon Jews had to adapt to the reality of exile and the loss of the Temple as the focal point of religious life. The main innovation was the introduction of the *beth midrash* (a study house, later known as a synagogue), which functioned both as a community and an adult education centre. Prayer does not appear to have played an important part in the proceedings in these centres until much later. Biblical prayer was a very personal process. The new emphasis on education was to have a far-reaching effect on the successful transition of Judaism from a national religion into an international one.

More than these practical developments, ideas about life and the universe affected Jewish thinking, particularly those of an apocalyptic nature. There is a very significant distinction between Isaiah's ideas of an ideal king exercising authority over a just and equitable kingdom and Daniel's vision, written in Babylon, of the 'End of Days'. Most traditional biblical commentators tended to see Daniel's visions as referring to the imminent arrival of Cyrus (who is referred to in the book as God's Messiah) and a possible return to Israel. This is consistent with the way in which they saw Isaiah's visions as being relatively short term, looking forward to the reformist reign of King Hezekiah.

Messianic intimations at this stage would have been limited to a return of the independent monarchy. The Bible uses the word *mashiach* (anointed) only in the context of an anointed priest. Later it was adapted to the appointment of a new king. After the destruction of the First Temple, it turned into a dream of the appointment of a king to rebuild the Davidic dynasty.

The language of the Jewish Babylonian book Daniel includes ideas and phrases that mark a significant departure from the Judean prophets and their writings. The complex angelology that appears in post-biblical Judaism owes a great deal to Babylonian culture. No angel was given a name in the Bible. The Hebrew word for 'angel' was identical to the word for 'messenger'. It is only after Babylon that angels with names appeared.

### THE SECOND COMMONWEALTH (500 BCE–70 CE)

The reformation carried out by Ezra nearly a hundred years after the first return consolidated a lot of the innovations of the exile. He reformed the priesthood to revive its role as the preserver of the religious tradition, rather than that of privileged aristocrats. His insistence on putting away foreign wives shows the transition from a national, tribal structure, into which one married and became automatically absorbed, into an ideologically driven community where commitment as much as birth determined membership.

Ezra was credited with adapting the institutions of the *mishmar* and adding that of the *ma'amad*. The mishmar is referred to in the Book of Chronicles and is traditionally ascribed to King David. The priests and Levites were divided administratively into 'clans' called a 'watch' or a mishmar. For two weeks each year, local areas sent rural priests and Levites up to Jerusalem to participate in the daily temple service (there must have been too many to be accommodated in Jerusalem and for all of them to be gainfully employed in the Temple full-time).

Ezra's innovation was to involve Israelites in the process. While those who could went up to Jerusalem, the local community gathered in their synagogues and studied what was happening in Jerusalem. The ma'amad was the term used to connect the local Israelites studying with those standing by in Jerusalem.

The study of Torah became institutionalised. Both regular readings and annual study programmes were designed to integrate two separate religious traditions, that of the priest and that of the layman. In this way, the synagogue, which remained an essential element of Diaspora survival, coexisted with temple worship in the re-established Jewish State. For the first time prayers were given an official format, even though they were not made obligatory until the destruction of the Second Temple.

The crucial innovation brought about by Ezra was to establish a community of scholars whose task it was to study and to teach the tradition, both in its written and in its oral form. This led eventually to a body of rabbis, a meritocracy drawn from the lower ranks of society, who were able to rise on the basis of their personal scholarship to a leadership position that rivalled that of the aristocratic priesthood. In time it led to the Sadducee/Pharisee schism.

## Sadducees and Pharisees

The Sadducees took their name from the dominant priestly family the House of Zadok. 'Zadoki' in its Grecian form became Sadducee. The Separatists were called precisely that, Parushim, which again in its Greek form became Pharisee. Ideologically the split developed both into a political one, nationalist as opposed to internationalist, and also into one over the Oral Law.

The Sadducees fought for the literal integrity of the written Torah. In contrast, the Pharisees elevated the oral Torah. The priesthood had a vested interest in limiting interpretation of holy texts because eventually this could lead to restrictions on their privileges, such as tithes and parts of sacrifices. The rabbis, on the other hand, saw the Oral Law as a way of caring for the weaker members of society, challenging sinecures and enthusing the community: 'a bastard who is a scholar takes precedence over a high priest who is an ignoramus,' says the Talmud.

The priesthood argued that the Oral Law was a rabbinic invention. The Samaritans supported them. The rabbis argued that there must always have been an Oral Law and that the prophetic tradition had preserved it in the face of priestly indifference or opposition.

Rabbinic thought took on a polemical character, which was designed both to refute Sadducee and Samaritan criticism but more importantly to educate the Judean laity in a more proactive and demanding religious life. The Temple remained the focal point of Jewish life despite the politicisation of the High Priesthood. But, in the Holy Land as well as in the Diaspora, study and extra-temple practice came to characterise Jewish life in general.

As the power of Persia gave way to Greek cultural expansion, 300 years before the Common Era, the Sadducees saw themselves as having more in common with the cosmopolitan Greeks than they did with their own poorer peasant population. They were responsible for introducing theatre, baths and circuses into Jerusalem. The more they tended towards Greek culture and attitudes, the more the Pharisees championed the national and cultural integrity of the Jewish tradition. If the Sadducees saw Greek rationalism as the correct mindset, the Pharisees were keen to establish mystical and non-rational dimensions of religious experience.

Just as the Philo-Greeks asserted international values, the Pharisees emphasised the importance of land and local institutions. Whatever disdain they held for the political priesthood, they accepted that ultimate religious authority and supremacy had to be vested in the Temple and Jerusalem. Despite their differences, throughout the Second Temple period the Pharisees accepted priestly control over the temple service but exerted pressure so that some accommodation took place. Given the Pharisees' control over the vast majority of the populace and over the Diaspora communities, they increasingly emerged as the major force for spiritual regeneration.

Yet, at the same time, the Jerusalem rabbinate was in competition with the Babylonian rabbinate for rabbinic supremacy. Babylon retained its Exilarch, the Reysh Galuta, who was the community head descended from the Davidic line. This position paralleled the head of the community in the Land of Israel, the Nasi, descended from the same family tree. The academic head in Babylon was called the Reysh Metivta. His role was the Babylonian equivalent of the head of the court, the Av Beth Din, in Judea. At various times there were periods of joint leadership, at others the Nasi ruled supreme. The tension between the two community heads often erupted into conflict.

The actual name of the territory occupied by the Jews varied both according to political changes and cultural ones. Judea, Palestine, Israel and later the Holy Land, all became synonymous for that relatively small territory that was the hub of Jewish existence from the return and for nearly a thousand years. In the Jewish literature of the time it was usually called *Eretz*

*Yisrael* (the Land of Israel), or in Babylon it was often referred to simply as 'the West'.

Towards the end of the Second Temple and the ultimate disappearance of the Sadducees, the Pharisees were left as the bearers of the rabbinic tradition and the term Pharisee fell into disuse. It was more appropriate, now, to allow the general term rav (literally 'master' or 'teacher') to replace the technical name Pharisee. But they were also known simply by their titles rebbi, rav or rabban depending on community custom. Sometimes the most famous were referred to only by their first names, as in the case of Hillel.

The rabbis were not a homogeneous group of men. They came from across the spectrum of Jewish life, from wealthy and poor backgrounds. Their constituency ranged from the Ganges to the Nile. Some of them were reformers advocating much of the agenda of the New Testament. But they saw themselves as being part of the wider Jewish world, loyal to its constitution, and, at that time, as being part of the largest and most impressive monotheistic movement in the world they inhabited.

Other divisions, both political and religious, played an important part in the development not only of Judaism but also other religious movements in the Middle East. On the one hand, the nationalist and anti-Roman movements led to schisms and rivalries (as do all liberation movements). On the other hand, the tendency to withdraw from society spawned a series of important sectarian innovations. The term the 'Dead Sea Sects' covers a wide range of groups, monastic, celibate and communitarian. Some were innovatively mystical, others loyal to tradition. Some groups created new texts and new interpretations of old ones. Others were apocalyptic or simply revolutionary. They and their creative writings helped spawn a range of new and fascinating ideas and religious approaches that influenced both Judaism and a range of emerging religious movements of the time.

## The Oral Law

It has always been a rabbinic assumption that the Written Law must have had an oral commentary. So that when a biblical ruling such as 'An Eye for Eye and tooth for a tooth' was given, a judge must have had some mechanism for dealing with situations such as when a toothless man broke the tooth of another. Or when Moses declared that on the Festival of Tabernacles one had to take 'the fruit of a pleasant tree' they must have had some more supplementary information to tell them what sort of tree it was. Nevertheless the Oral Law became an essential element in the expansion of Judaism from its biblical origins.

During the 500-year period of the Second Commonwealth, as it is often called, the Jews achieved a great measure of self-rule even if they were subject to the political control of Persia and then Greece (in its various forms), and finally the Roman Empire. As a result, the biblical constitution that dealt with every aspect of a nation's life was developed and expanded to meet new and problematic conditions. Remaining loyal to the text, the rabbis constantly expanded and interpreted the biblical laws relying upon what they argued were four legitimate methods sanctioned by the oral tradition. The first two, textual comparisons and 'principles of deduction', established the parameters of textual analysis. There were several alternative schemas, but ultimately they were reduced to thirteen that are to this day read at each morning service.

The third element was tradition. The phrase 'from Moses on Sinai' accounted for interpretations or innovations that had been current for so long that they were assumed to have been contemporaneous with the original revelation. Finally, there was outright rabbinic innovation, designed to protect and strengthen the spirit and the practice of the original revelation, creating 'fences around the law'.

The role of the rabbis as the primary transmitters of tradition to the nation (as opposed to the purely functionary role now ascribed to the priests) meant that they became in effect the legislative as well as the spiritual authorities and teachers. Through the process of *midrash*, exegetical and homiletic interpretation of scriptures, they conveyed the ethical and spiritual tradition of Judaism. Through *Halacha* (Law), they continued the process of developing biblical law through the new cultural and economic circumstances they faced. This body of knowledge, law and lore, known as the Oral Law, was originally intended to be exactly that, oral and not written. 'That which is written must not be transmitted orally and that which is oral may not be written down.' Later factors would change this.

It would be wrong to think that authority went unchallenged. Apart from the sectarians who withdrew from the mainstream communities and the Sadducees who remained opposed to the rabbinic process, within the rabbinic camp itself there were different schools. Hillel, born a Babylonian, had become the greatest authority of the era before the destruction of the Temple. He was an outstanding legislator and teacher. His popular maxim, 'what is hateful to you, do not do to your neighbour' (*Avot* 1.6), was later borrowed and adapted by other groups. He was particularly egalitarian in his approach. He was urbane and open-minded.

Hillel contrasted with his great aristocratic contemporary Shammai, who emphasised a more rigidly academic and authoritarian approach. Both saw education as crucial to religious survival. Hillel, in particular, sought to bridge the gap opening up between the educated and the ignorant. There was as much a rebellious and an innovatory mood within the rabbinic camp as there was an authoritarian one. Both Hillel and Shammai set up their own academies to rival the older established ones in Judea and Babylonia, and after the deaths of their founders these schools continued to debate the essential issues of Jewish law in all its ramifications as a national constitution.

This debate was not only on matters of Halacha. For two years they argued over the issue of whether it was better for man to have been created or not. They finally agreed that it would have been better had man not been made, but they added a coda that since he was created, he must be positive and find the right way to behave. On occasion the schools came together to vote and determine an agreed agenda; in general, the school of Hillel tended to win but not always. The rabbinic tradition emphasised the importance of genuine disagreement and the need to retain minority opinions. These two schools exerted a long and profound influence on the rabbinic traditions.

## The Talmudic Era (70 CE–500 CE)

The Roman Wars signalled the death of the old Temple order and later, under Hadrian, the end of the Judean community. Rabban Yochanan ben Zakkai, the acknowledged head of the rabbinic community, had given up the fight to retain Jerusalem. The internal schisms were so deep that he despaired of reconciling them. In particular, he distanced himself from the extreme nationalists ready to fight to the last man. He withdrew from Jerusalem. He negotiated terms with Vespasian and retired to Yavneh on the coastal plain where he was allowed to re-establish rabbinic authority even as the Romans finished off their campaign against the nationalists in Jerusalem. Important as the land and Jerusalem was to them, the mainstream Pharisees saw a bigger picture and wider goals that needed to be pursued. Besides, they had a wider remit than the embattled extremists in Judea and Galilee.

The generation after the destruction took momentous decisions to preserve Jewish traditions in the wake of the total disappearance of the temple service. After all, for the first 1,500 years and more of the Jewish religion, sacrifices and temple worship had been the essential feature of public worship.

For Jews the Temple and sacrifices became emblematic of the past and their loss a reminder of the pain of exile. They accepted for themselves and the community a general state of mourning that included fasts, a ban on music, eating food with ashes, leaving parts of homes uncompleted, and remembering the destruction at every wedding and before every meal.

The primary way in which the temple service was replaced was through prayer. The rabbis introduced communal prayers to replace the sacrificial system. Some of this had already begun informally during the Babylonian exile and in the ongoing Diaspora, but now it became enshrined by formal diktat. Biblical prayer was always and remained personal and informal. The prayers that were introduced now were communal and fixed. Together with study of the Torah in both its oral and written forms, this became the new expression of divine service. Now more than ever the Jews were 'the people of the book'. One can see from the writings of Maimonides that the issue of whether sacrifices would one day return or not was an ongoing debate within Judaism, but of course now it was largely academic.

The decision was taken to start writing down the oral laws and traditions before they could be lost in the ongoing persecutions and political upheavals. The process had begun around the time of the destruction of the Temple. The collapse of the Bar Cochba Revolution in 135 CE brought about more destruction of rabbinic life, in particular the school of Rabbi Akiva, the prototype of a rabbinic leader, a self-motivated shepherd turned academic, who had been extremely popular and revered. Sadly, his political views in supporting Bar Cochba as the messiah were disastrous for the whole community. He was killed, as were most of his pupils.

The head of the community Judah the Prince (Rabbi Yehuda HaNassi) took the decision to write down and compile the Oral law into what became known as the *Mishna*. There had been earlier collections notably by Rabbi Meir, but Judah the Prince's comprehensive Mishna became the authoritative text.

## The Talmud

The Mishna was a six-volume compilation of the decisions and discussions that had taken place both about biblical law and rabbinic interpretation and innovation. Its sections dealt with Civil Law and Politics, Marriage and Divorce, Agriculture, Daily Life, Ritual and Authority, Purity, and Sacrifices. It reflected the whole gamut of life as any constitution would.

No sooner had the Mishna appeared than the academies of Israel and Babylon began to analyse and often challenge both its substance and its form. There were other traditions, conflicting texts called *Beraitot*, and incorrect attributions and scribal errors. This discussion on the Mishna was called the *Gemara*. There would in time be two Gemaras, a Jerusalem and a Babylonian. Together the Mishna and the Gemara were given the general name of the Talmud. It has dominated Jewish religious life ever since.

It would be true to say that the Talmud became in many ways even more important than the Bible as a repository of Jewish law and custom. Talmudic interpretation consciously tried to differentiate the Jewish Bible from the Christian as much as possible. The Talmud became the means of Jewish religious survival and resurrection over the coming 400 years as slowly all but a few embers of Jewish life were extinguished from the ancestral lands.

Another important decision at the time was the fixing of the canon of the biblical books. There had been a series of texts that claimed authority. Some were apocalyptic, such as the Book of Enoch and the Book of Jubilees. There were books known as 'wisdom literature', such Ecclesiasticus or *Ben Sirach*, and others were regarded as simply political, such as the Books of the Maccabees. They were included in the Christian Bible as the Apocrypha, but excluded from the Jewish canon.

The Dead Sea sects had produced a significant body of texts of a ritual as well as a homiletic nature. There was a corpus of mystical works, the *Hechalot* literature, which sought to understand the Chambers of the Divine Palace, and the *Shiur Koma* literature, which described the unique mystical connection between man and God empowering both with a degree of similar characteristics. These were considered by many to be as important as other texts such as Daniel, Ecclesiastes, or even the Song of Songs.

The rabbinic decision to exclude the Apocryphal books and to relegate mystical works to a lower level of sanctity had the effect of reinforcing mainstream Judaism against the mystics, the apocalyptics and Graeco-Roman ideologies. All of these continued to play a part in the development of Jewish life, but they were marginalised to a large degree by the canonisation of the Jewish Bible.

Although the threat from the Sadducees had now gone, the priests had been left with a very limited symbolical role (ironically confined almost exclusively to the synagogue), and their ideology and that of the Samaritans coalesced in time into a new threat to rabbinic authority. The Christian schism became an external threat after Constantine, but Karaism (or Karaitism), the ideology of accepting the written law only and not the oral law, became the major internal conflict within Judaism over the next thousand years. In this turbulent, creative period, it was the rabbinic interpretation of the biblical texts as opposed to any and all of the others that defined mainstream Judaism.

The Jerusalem Talmud reflected the declining state of the Jewish community in Jerusalem. It was compiled in about 350 CE. The larger and authoritative Babylonian Talmud was complied in about 500 CE by Ravina and Rav Ashi. It was a massive work of over 63 sections based on the categories and books of the Mishna. In addition, extra collections of Minor Tractates, the *Tosefta*, and a whole host of commentaries both legal and exegetical make up the present printed text of the Talmud as it is studied throughout the Jewish world. The Jewish talmudic academies, called *metivtot* or *yeshivot*, then and to this day, varied in the way they studied the Talmud, some going for great depth and detail, others for breadth and themes. But they all made the study complex and demanding, and in many cases a lifetime's work.

Within the Talmud itself one can distinguish three separate but interwoven categories of subject matter. There is Halacha, essentially law, but covering the complete gamut of life, personal, communal and national. Then there is Midrash, which deals with the interpretation of biblical texts but is also the vehicle of what one might call theological discussion and preaching to the wider audiences. It is consciously not in the rational, philosophical style of Christian theology. Finally, *Aggadata* contains traditions, of folklore, folk medicine, and traditions of a historical and social nature, issues such as medicinal remedies, the interpretation of dreams, and magic.

In effect, the Talmud is a record of Jewish religious life and culture spanning the thousand years from the end of the biblical era till the end of the talmudic era. The work is encyclopaedic and not always systematic. There are so many conflicting ideas to be found in the Talmud on almost every topic that it is no exaggeration to say that for every talmudic maxim or opinion, one can almost certainly find its opposite. This is part of the charm, and the frustration, of a work that is consciously not scientific.

The Talmuds define Judaism as a way of life rather than a theological system. It is not possible to understand the development of Judaism without delving into the Talmud to understand the minds and decisions of the rabbis who oversaw its transition from a tradition that revolved around the Temple in Jerusalem, to a way of life that could adapt to life in almost any climate of opinion or regime.

A further piece in the talmudic jigsaw was the role of the Massoretes. Their name comes from the Hebrew *Masorah* which means a received tradition. They were rabbis who specialised in validating and standardising texts, both biblical and post-biblical. They were linguists. They studied grammar and literary structure in the received traditions. It is to them that Judaism owes the standardised texts of its Holy Writ as read today.

## Talmudic Theology

The theology of the Talmud is fascinating in that it is primarily a polemic, a teaching vehicle, anxious to assert certain core ideas, but, more importantly, eager to counteract certain negative ones. It seems consciously to limit the number of positive belief requirements and focus on combating antagonistic or nihilistic ones. It sees its main opponent as the pagan, epicurean free-for-all. Although the Talmud is not ascetic in general, it encourages participation in and enjoyment of the pleasures of life, but it also preaches restraint.

There is no formulation of a set credo or list of required beliefs in the Talmud. But there are indeed certain essential accepted ideas. The most often reiterated is that of revelation as referring specifically to the Torah, in both its written and oral forms. There is no attempt to prove the existence of God, but God is accepted as the ultimate power and force behind the universe, the power to which all humans should submit themselves and the power that rewards and punishes human beings for their actions. There is a great deal of discussion about how God rewards or punishes. Of course, this is implicit in the biblical formulation of the Ten Principles (known inaccurately as the Ten Commandments). But the vicissitudes of life made it very hard to understand the mind of God.

One of the favourite ways of dealing with the issue of God's relation to humanity was the belief that reward and punishment may not be executed in this world but in the next. This was not a unanimously accepted idea, but it is a recurrent one. Similarly, the idea of resurrection of the soul is debated in various places in the Talmud, but it is left unclear exactly what is the distinction between resurrection and the afterlife and whether resurrection happens in this world or the next. It is even possible to understand some talmudic passages as proposing an eastern concept of the unity of all life, whether before or after death.

The Talmud has many references to the Messiah, but here too the concept is not defined. There is Messiah the Son of David, Messiah the Son of Joseph, Elijah and a debate as to whether the Messianic Era has come or not, and whether it is a supernatural state or simply a state of improved human behaviour.

These ideas are circulated as opinions, not as defined theological concepts. The main source for these ideas, the last chapter of the Tractate *Sanhedrin* in the Babylonian Talmud, starts off with the mishnaic formula that 'everyone has a place in the World to Come but these do not: someone who says that Resurrection is not found in the Torah, someone who rejects the idea of Revelation on Sinai, an epicurean etc.' The very negative formulation underlines the fact that the rabbis were more concerned to refute the atheists as opposed to the agnostics. Doubt was acceptable, but certainty in a negative way was regarded as pagan arrogance.

It is easier to talk about ideas that the talmudic rabbis disagree with than about exactly how Jewish belief should be formulated. The rabbis were primarily concerned with behaviour. It was the public rejection of religious law that put someone beyond the pale, rather than the inability to formulate positive theological truths.

To a large extent this emphasis on behaviour enabled Judaism to survive under different and often conflicting cultural and ideological situations. By leaving ideas open to interpretation, it offered a flexibility that contrasted with the need for ritual conformity. This ritual conformity enabled Diaspora Jews from around the world to share much more than their different intellectual ideas might have enabled them to do.

For all its concern with Jewish survival, the Talmud looks at the non-Jewish world through remarkably progressive eyes. Pious non-Jews have a part in the world to come. Despite the resistance to Greek culture, there are many stories of debates and exchanges between the rabbis and Roman leaders and intellectuals. It is true that the Talmud sees Jewish law as conveying certain rights and privileges on its adherents, but these could be extended to non-Jews at will and as circumstances permitted. The issue was whether a non-Jew subscribed to a moral code and behaved in an ethical way. The opposition to paganism was not so much to its theological propositions but rather to its absence of morality and ethical behaviour.

Although Judaism did expect that everyone would follow its very demanding standards, this did not mean that Judaism had no interest in what the non-Jewish world did, or how it behaved religiously. There were seven Noachide laws that if adhered to by a non-Jew would render him or her one of the 'Pious of the Nations of the World'. These laws stated that one had to respect God, not worship idols, not murder, not commit adultery, not steal, not be cruel to animals and, finally, one had to establish courts of law.

The old biblical laws demanding the destruction of the surrounding peoples were interpreted out of existence on the grounds that the old peoples mentioned in the Bible could no longer be identified after the Assyrian king Sennacharib had invaded the area in 720 BCE and displaced them all. Even the hated tribe of Amalek was no longer identifiable, nor were the biblically prohibited tribes of Moab and Ammon. The biblical Egyptians were believed to have disappeared, and the current inhabitants of Egypt were another people altogether. The ideal was peaceful coexistence with surrounding peoples wherever one was, and the hope that they would adhere to a basic moral and religious code.

The Bible had already emphasised the importance of studying the commandments and teaching them. The Talmud, likewise, became not an esoteric text for scholars or priests alone but a popular source of instruction and analysis. Study was placed together with prayer as the way to serve God, even more so since the Temple no longer existed. By making the Talmud the popular educational vehicle for everyone, the rabbis ensured the continuity of a learned laity and established both the meritocratic and egalitarian nature of Jewish religious if not social life.

By the time the Babylonian Talmud had been completed, the old order had gone. Israel no longer was a centre of Jewish learning, although small communities continued to hold on both around Jerusalem and in Galilee, and the Jerusalem authorities still reserved the right to fix the calendar, although this became an issue with some Diaspora communities. Authority on religious matters was increasingly vested in the local rabbinate, and various schools of customs and traditions made centralised authority less appropriate. Nevertheless, great experts were acknowledged wherever they happened to live and were consulted across the political boundaries.

The *Saboraim* and the *Geonim*, the great heads of the Baylonian academies, were the next generation of masters. The old distinction between the communities of the East (Babylon) and the West (Israel) was now drawn between Jews living in the Roman Empire (as far west as Spain) and those living under the Eastern Empires. Soon this became a distinction between those living under Christianity and those living under Islam.

New waves of religious creativity began to emerge, in particular the philosophical, theological tradition that contrasted with the mystical or kabbalistic. But whatever changes and upheavals occurred, the force of the Halacha, the Jewish religious structure, was the common agenda and binding force that kept all Jewish communities, wherever they were, together. It was constantly being tested by new situations and challenges and continued to develop.

The Talmud had left many legal issues open and so the debates did not end. Each generation needed to update its legislative programmes, just as each community added on its own customs and variations. Nothing stood still and the constant study ensured that the tradition continued to develop.

# Chapter 3

# A Theological Overview: 2

## POST-TALMUDIC ERA (500 CE–1500 CE)

The rise of Christianity and Islam with their rival schools of theology exerted a powerful influence on Judaism. Philo of Alexandria in the first century had been the first to seek to explain Judaism to Roman society, but he had not, it appears, known much Hebrew and he was uniquely Alexandrian. The mainstream rabbinic leaders had contact with Roman thinkers and were called upon to justify themselves and Judaism as the Talmud testifies in many places. But the Talmud itself records no examples of philosophical thinking.

As the other religions started using philosophy to defend and attack, Jews began to respond in kind. Aristotelian and Platonic thought patterns and systems came to dominate all theological discourse. Hard as many authorities within Judaism tried to resist this trend, it inevitably had its effects.

One of the last leaders of Babylonian Jewry Saadya Gaon (882–942) fought for Jewish intellectual survival on two fronts. The Kaarite schism, which denied the validity of the Oral Law, rabbinic authority and innovations, was proving more persistent than expected. The Kaarites, successors in many ways of the Saduccees, far from disappearing, were actually challenging for the leadership of the Jewish community. Saadya had to argue the case that rabbinic Judaism was indeed the heir to the biblical tradition and was not a later 'invention'. It is largely due to him that the rival claim was defeated and slowly sank into insignificance.

Just as challenging to Judaism were the claims of Christianity and Islam that only they could be considered 'real' religions, for only they had coherent theological systems. Saadya's great work *Emunot VeDeot* (*Beliefs and Principles*) was the best known major philosophical justification of Judaism to appear since Philo of Alexandria interpreted the Bible in a way that made it accessible to the philosophical mind of his day. Saadyah's was almost the last breath of the great Babylonian tradition, and after him the Gaonate began to decline and Jewish creativity moved westward.

Centres in Italy and North Africa grew and produced important institutions and leaders. But it was in Muslim Spain, under the Umayyads in Cordova particularly, that Jewish life and scholarship next really flourished. A whole class of Jewish 'civil servants' emerged, men like Hasdai Ibn Shaprut, who served from 912–976, Samuel HaNaggid (993–1069) and Solomon Ibn Gabirol (1021–1069), as well as great thinkers and scholars.

Yehuda Halevy (1086–1167) argued the case for Judaism in his great book *The Kuzari*. It was based on the story of the Caucasian tribe, the Khazars, who had converted to Judaism. It was a powerful philosophical as well as poetic argument that emphasised the national element in distinguishing Judaism from the other monotheistic traditions. He imagined the Khazar king consulting, debating and testing Jewish, Christian and Muslim representatives before deciding that Judaism was the religion he preferred. Halevy particularly emphasised the love of Zion and his poetry, expressing his love for the Land of Israel, exerted tremendous influence on attitudes to the Land of Israel over the next millennium. His line 'My heart is in the East but I am at the farthest edge of the West' became an anthem for Jews as they dreamed of their ancient self-determination. His contemporary Abraham Ibn Ezra was an outstanding thinker, commentator and scholar. His theological work *Foundation of Fear* was a seminal influence on the medieval world. Together with Halevy, he resurrected the Hebrew language as a vehicle of literary and philosophical expression.

## Maimonides

Maimonides (1135–1204), known as RaMBaM, the acrostic of Rabbi Moses Ben Maimon, was the next giant of Jewish thought. Born in Cordova in Spain in an Islamic society he fled the new intolerant Muslim Almohide regime and eventually moved to Egypt where he gained fame as a physician. His great philosophical work *The Guide to the Perplexed*, written originally in Arabic, was a magisterial attempt to reconcile Judaism with Aristotelian philosophy and show that Judaism could indeed offer a theological system the equal of any other.

Many rabbis attacked this work on the grounds that Judaism should have no truck at all with Greek ideas and make no attempt to ape the Christian or Muslim theologians. So great was the antagonism that his books were banned and even burnt in some quarters. His philosophy was banned by the great RashBa, Rabbi Shlomo Ben Aderet of Barcelona (1235–1310). Even then, Judaism was divided between those who were prepared to study and engage with other disciplines and those who refused to.

Rambam was attacked from another angle by philosophers such as Ibn Daud (1110–1180), Hasdai Crescas (1350–1412), and Joseph Albo (c.1390–1450). They objected to his *Thirteen Principles of Faith*. This was an attempt to provide a popular 'credo' of Judaism, something that hitherto rabbis had been reluctant to do. After all, if the Talmud itself did not compile a thorough list of prescribed beliefs, why should it be done now?

The *Ten Principles of Faith* that Maimonides formulated included the ideas of God as the creator and His unity, His incorporeality, His eternality and that He is the only object of worship. They insisted on the truth of the Sinai Revelation, the divine and immutable nature of the Torah and the authority of Moses and the prophetic tradition, divine benevolence and omniscience, resurrection and the coming of the Messiah. All of these ideas were indeed to be found within the tradition, but not in a defined or structured way.

Joseph Albo did not deny the importance of the principles. He simply thought that they could not be described as dogmas, necessary beliefs. There were only three essentials, he argued, Divinity, Revelation and Benevolence. Nevertheless, Maimonides' principles gained currency over time; they became the simple menu of traditional Jewish beliefs and were incorporated into the prayer book and services, both in prose and poetry.

Maimonides was also a great Halachist (jurist), and it is in this realm that his influence remains powerful to this day. He was the most widely read Halachist producing a popular compendium of laws and customs based on the developments that followed the end of the talmudic era. It is true to say that a major new code of Jewish law has been published virtually every 500 years. However, they all refer back to earlier codes and the *Yad HaChazaka* of Maimonides is still a basic text for Jewish law today, although its authority carries more weight with the Sepharadi communities than with the Ashkenazi ones.

Spain was the crucible of most creative Jewish literature. Islamic Spain was a cultural paradise for the Jews where they could study and participate in society as well. The early Middle Ages in Spain were regarded as a Golden Age. Even the Christian north was influenced by proximity to the Muslim provinces. But as a different form of Islam took over and then retreated and a more aggressive Christianity replaced it, Spain became similar to the rest of Europe.

Medieval Europe was not entirely the dark, primitive and violent world it is often described as. There was a great deal of spiritual creativity. As well as the increase in philosophy, there was also a tremendous outpouring of other kinds of scholarship. The Jews were excluded from the great European universities, which all started out as theological colleges of training for the priesthood. As a result, they were forced to develop their own scholarship parallel to that of the Christian and Muslim worlds.

From Spain to the Rhineland, from Italy up into southern France, centres of Jewish scholarship flourished despite the constant hazards of expulsion, crusades, massacres and expropriation. Great commentators such as Rashi (1040–1105) and Nachmanides (1194–1270) extended the boundaries of Jewish learning along the familiar tracks of bible commentary, Halacha and thought. But there was another parallel world, the world of mysticism and magic. Just as alchemy and sorcery coexisted with mainstream Christianity in the West and Islam in the East, so too in medieval Jewry esoteric and alternative areas of experiment, folk traditions and secret study coexisted with the mainstream religious activities.

## Mysticism
Scholars still argue about the origins of the mystical tradition called the Kabbalah. The term itself as applied to mystical literature did not occur until

the first millennium. However the Talmud discusses the esoteric world and refers in Tractate *Chagigah* to types of knowledge that should not be taught to everyone (as opposed to the revealed Torah, which was indeed for everyone).

The first chapter of Ezekiel is the source of this secret tradition, but the term used in the Talmud is *Maaseh Merkava* (the business of the chariot). This hints back to the chariot of fire that took the prophet Elijah up to Heaven (2 Kings 2). Certain rabbis of the Talmud had a reputation for esoteric expertise, notably Rabbi Shimon Bar Yochai in the second century, who had to hide in a cave from the Romans for twelve years. According to legend, wherever Shimon Bar Yochai sat and studied, flames encircled him. Fire became a metaphor in talmudic language for the mystical.

The rabbis of the Talmud felt that mystical knowledge and power was too dangerous a tool to be available to everyone indiscriminately and insisted that it should only be studied by a select few sitting at the feet of trusted and recognised masters. Of course, in the centuries before the millennium and during the formative period of the Mishna, a great deal of esoteric literature and many mystical groups flourished both within and without the main-stream tradition. Some of the earliest texts of the Kabbalah, *Sefer Yetzira* and *Sefer Bahir*, may even have dated from this period. But the real expansion of the mystical tradition coincides with a general era of interest in esoteric reli-gion that can be found in Christianity and Islam in the medieval period. Despite the Crusades and the political rivalry, a great deal of cross-cultural fertilisation was taking place.

Jewish study was divided into these areas. *Niglah* (the revealed) included the biblical and talmudic texts and all aspects of Halacha, Midrash and Aggadah. Philosophy occupied a category of its own, which was not univer-sally accepted and certainly not a popular field of study. Finally, *Nistar* (the secret body of knowledge) was the term used for esoteric, mystical study of the sort that would come to be known as Kabbalah, literally 'the received tradition'.

The body of writing that came to be known as Kabbalah was divided into three areas. The first was purely abstract. It was a framework for under-standing the world, creation, and divine intervention in ways that were intentionally not bound by the conventions of philosophical thought. It was essentially Jewish in that it expressed complete loyalty to the talmudic, halachic tradition and, initially, used the talmudic language and conventions.

Secondly, there was practical Kabbalah that wanted to find ways of actu-ally encountering the Divine, of using divine power to create life, alter reality and give one knowledge that others might not have. In some ways, this was rather like the role alchemy played in the Christian world. However, the 'secret' was primarily the secret of knowing how to harness divine creative energy. The primary practical goal of this was to try and reproduce human life. Medieval rabbinic literature has many discussions about the legal status of such a creation. But, apart from the famous myth of the Golem of Prague (attributed to the great Rabbi Judah Loew, who died in 1609), there is no objective evidence that anyone succeeded.

Finally, there was astrological and magical Kabbalah that sought to ease the pain of the suffering and the insecure by providing a simple scheme that explained the physical world. Often this was done in terms of another system to that asserted by formal religion, namely in folk culture such as astrology.

A tremendous amount of literature began to emerge in all these areas and it was not in any way considered initially a challenge to the established religious authorities for it was seen as an area of advanced knowledge that only the best and the brightest of the students would enter into once the basics had been mastered.

Abraham Abulafia (1240–1292), born in Saragossa, and his pupil Joseph Gikatilla (1248–1325) wrote important books and commentaries on mainstream Kabbalah and also generated interest in holistic practices very similar to eastern traditions. But outstanding mainstream authorities like Nachmanides (1194–1270) or much later the Gaon of Vilna (1720–1797), despite their opposition to popular mystical fashions, were also major experts in theoretical Kabbalah. Indeed, when Nachmanides was called upon to defend Judaism against the Dominicans in the disputation of Barcelona in 1263, debate focused on the question of whether Kabbalah was an essential part of Judaism.

With the appearance of the *Zohar*, the great mystical work that is both a commentary on the Torah and a series of lectures on mystical themes, Kabbalah took its place alongside traditional texts. There remains controversy to this day as to whether Moses De Leon (1250–1305) actually wrote the Zohar, compiled it or simply discovered the long lost text attributed to the second century authority Simon Bar Yochai who is the stated author. Traditionalists accept the earlier authorship and it has acquired a status in the Jewish literary tradition to the point where some study every day a part of the Torah, the Mishna, the Gemara and the Zohar. In the Sepharadi world, in particular, the Zohar has always exerted a profound influence.

After the expulsion from Spain in 1492, a tide of exceptionally talented Jews swept eastward back across the Mediterranean to the Land of Israel, and to the city of Safed in particular. The kabbalistic approach to Judaism influenced the greatest rabbis of the succeeding generations. Safed, in Upper Galilee, was home to a reconstructed Spanish Jewish community. It included outstanding scholars such as Joseph Caro (1488–1575), whose great work the *Shulchan Aruch* (*The Table Laid*) was a summation of the halachic development of Judaism over the previous 1,000 years since the end of the talmudic era.

But Safed was also the centre of Kabbalah. It was the home of the innovative Moses Cordovero (1522–1570) and of Isaac Luria (1534–1572), the *Ari'zal* (or lion) as he is known, one of the giants of the mystical tradition. He and his school, men like Chaim Vital (1542–1620), who transcribed his teachings, were responsible for making Kabbalah more accessible. They used it as a way of adding dimensions to the ritual structure of Judaism, combining it with meditation, contemplation, song and dance, overturning the solemn traditions that harked back to the pain of the destruction of the Temple and exile. They established norms of religious behaviour that led to a more charismatic and popular expression of ecstatic Judaism. This in turn produced a Messianic fervour that expected divine intervention at any moment. Luria's influence on prayer and worship was probably greater than any person's since the great era of post-Destruction Judaism.

## NEW CHALLENGES (1600 CE–2000 CE)

### Chassidism

Although over time the main centres of Kabbalah developed in the east and in North Africa, it was the animating spirit of one of the most important changes in European Jewish life, the Chassidic revolution. In Eastern Europe Jewish communities were now in a parlous state. Poverty and dispersion had taken many Jews into rural isolation. In the main cities rabbinic authority remained strong, but poverty created a social division between the rich and the poor, the learned and the ignorant.

The Cossack invasions of Poland in the seventeenth century were cataclysmic. The Chmielnicki massacres of 1648–1649 eroded what little security and confidence was left. The desire for a miracle was so strong that many looked to false Messiahs, Sabbatai Zevi (1626–1676), who was initially a serious Kabbalist but then converted to Islam, or Jacob Frank, a charlatan, to relieve them and when they failed, morale sunk even further.

Out of this depressed state emerged a charismatic popular leader, the Baal Shem Tov (1700–1760). The term *Baal Shem*, literally having a name, a reputation, was a generic one indicating someone who had special, usually kabbalistic powers of healing. Israel Baal Shem Tov was a travelling preacher who inspired depressed communities with his positive message of ecstasy and experience, rather than scholarship and formality. His brand of popular Judaism brought hope to millions of disadvantaged Jews and his movement, known as Chassidism (the movement of the Pious) spread throughout the east.

The greatest of the mainstream rabbis, the Gaon of Vilna, mistrusted this popular movement. He banned it. The anti-Chassidic movement was known as the *Mitnagdim*, the opponents. Western European communities also resisted the wilder, less rational approach of Chassidism. Nevertheless, the differences between them were marginal. Both communities adhered more or less to Halacha; the Chassidim were more flexible and relaxed about the details.

The Chassidic movement was not really a revolution in the sense that it tried to change or oppose the traditional halachic structure of Jewish life; but it put the emphasis on mystical experience, rather than on arid scholarship or dry conformity to rigid rules of behaviour. Ecstatic prayer and song and access to one's pious *rebbe* (a title reserved only for Chassidic masters) were open to everyone, regardless of background or lack of knowledge.

Soon there were rival synagogues in each community. The Chassidim adopted the Luria traditions of song and liturgical variations. It was known as *Nusach Sephard*, the style of Spain, to which it owed its origins (but was distinct from the main Sepharadi Eastern communities), as opposed to the main European tradition known as *Nusach Ashkenaz*.

The Chassidim also made a point of not trying to be like their non-Jewish neighbours. They took pride in appearing and dressing as differently as possible to the world around them, making no concessions to Western culture, which they saw as antithetic to their true and pure expression of ecstatic Judaism.

There were unique, individual masters like the Maggid of Mezeritch (1704–1772) and Nachman of Bratslav (1772–1811). In almost every town in Eastern Europe there were Chassidic miracle workers and often, great teachers and preachers.

Slowly the different leaders established their own dynasties. This meant that there was soon no more room for charismatic, self-made innovators and the Chassidic movement began to lose a great deal of its innovative creativity. Outstanding teachers and spiritual leaders continued to emerge, who often founded new 'sects'. But the initial iconoclasm soon cooled. The expansion of the movement itself was based on areas of habitation. People belonged or joined as much out of local convenience as out of devotion to a particular ideology. Ger was in Poland, Satmar in Hungary, and Lubavitch was in Russia. Over time, the different Chassidic dynasties became the equivalent of the different monastic orders in the Catholic Church, rivalling each other and claiming superiority. In general, by the nineteenth century, Chassidism became as entrenched and structured as the very system it set out to challenge. Nevertheless, it was Chassidism that kept the spirit and study of Kabbalah alive in the West.

If Kabbalah was so important and widespread, why did it acquire an aura of unreliability, even suspicion? The rabbinic response to the failed Sabbatai Zevi Messianic movement was to blame the Kabbalah for encouraging heterodox attitudes. The excesses of Jacob Frank and his followers (who believed that sexual freedom was an analogy for union with God) made matters worse. In the West the Enlightenment had enthroned rationalism so that all forms of mysticism were suspect, and the established Mitnaged rabbinate considered the study of Kabbalah by the masses a danger because it would encourage Chassidic tendencies. This defensiveness of the rabbinate was to be reinforced by two other trends.

## The Haskalla

Slowly Jews in Europe found ways of escaping the physical and cultural ghettos they had been forced into and started to challenge the social and religious anti-Semitism that characterised Christian Europe. The collapse of the old empires and the fragmentation of Christianity helped, but there were still formidable obstacles to overcome. Judaism and Jews wherever they lived were considered inferior and a threat to the established hegemony.

Moses Mendelssohn (1729–1786) and Naftali Wessely (1725–1806) were the inspiration behind a move to relate Judaism to a secular, modern world. Moses Mendelssohn was one of the first Jews allowed to live in Berlin. He became a philosopher of note and a friend of the intellectual elite of the European academic and social world. He argued forcefully and effectively for a reassessment of the Jewish religion. He sought to show that it was not a primitive religion that had been overtaken by new revelations. In particular, his debates with the Christian theologian Lavater were vigorous and effective polemics in favour of Judaism. He translated the Bible into German and advocated opening up Jewish scholarship to other intellectual disciplines. Despite his own commitment to traditional Jewish life, the attractions of society drew his children away from Judaism with the result that he soon became a symbol to the eastern Jews of the dangers of a secular education.

As Napoleon moved eastward and extended Jewish emancipation, more and more Jews were attracted by the new opportunities. Even in Eastern Europe, amongst the intensely Jewish communities, the stirring of new knowledge and new horizons offered hopes of escape from the backward poverty that characterised the life of most Jews. The more the eastern Jewish rabbinate felt the pressure pulling them towards modernity, the more they felt the need to pull in the opposite direction.

The general term for this new movement to encourage secular learning was the *Haskallah* (the enlightenment). It affected Jewish life in two ways. It allowed many Jews to acquire a secular education, but this also led to greater assimilation. On the other, hand it pushed Jewish religious life in the opposite direction, a far cry from the Golden Age of Spain where Jews had participated in the life of the realm, yet remained loyal to their own values.

Another by-product of Haskalla was the conscious attempt of the Yeshiva world, the traditional schools for further Jewish religious study to raise their own academic level to compete with the universities. Rabbi Chayim of Volozhin initiated a new trend in 1803 by establishing academic centres with a very high level of intellectual rigour, yet devoted exclusively to the analysis of Jewish texts. The great academies of Volozhon and later Mir, Ponevez and Slabodka in Lithuania, came to exercise a profound influence on the nature of Jewish life in the East where study became the essential tool for Jewish progress and survival.

## Reform Judaism

In the West the challenge of modernity led to the Reform movement in the first half of the nineteenth century. Abraham Geiger (1810–1874) was the leading spirit of this new trend. Initially Reform had meant simply introducing the vernacular into the synagogues. Then it became an issue of how much of the *Wissenchaft*, the academic, scientific study of Judaism, should be incorporated into Jewish religious thinking. But, over time, it became a process of adjusting Jewish practice and attitudes to different cultures.

Initial 'reforms' were not far-reaching enough and a new more radical 'Liberal' movement developed in Germany in the mid-nineteenth century. Whereas in the past adjustments to the outside world had been made in the intellectual sphere, now it began to affect the way Halacha could be modified or jettisoned to suit the demands of a different society. Hitherto Judaism had survived by refusing to compromise on its practice. Now some Jews introduced the organ into their synagogues, with mixed choirs and other features of Christian services. Slowly the Reform movement moved further and further away from traditional practice. Abandoning traditional ideology was not such a threat to the integrity of the Jewish people as was the rejection of the law that had bound them together for so long. Reform was also a strongly patriotic movement in which citizenship came first and Judaism second. Reform movements began to remove references to Zion, as well as to the ancient sacrificial rites and to theological ideas they found archaic.

Whatever the differing ideologies or local conditions that had caused division within Jewish life over the previous 1,500 years, for the first time new ideologies emerged that threatened the behavioural and constitutional integrity of the Jewish people. The trouble was that it convinced the traditionalists that only by remaining impervious to external ideas could they retain their cohesion and guarantee survival. It led to a frame of mind that saw anything secular as a threat, and any lightening of the strictness of law as a sign of weakness. The attempt to introduce a modified secular programme into the study at Volozhyn (supported by a minority of rabbis) led to the closure of the yeshiva altogether. The great Moses Sofer (1762–1839), known from his nom de plume as the Chatam Sofer, born in Frankfurt but later the Rabbi of Pressburg, came to exercise a profound influence on mainstream Central European Jewry. He argued that any new development was dangerous and all new or secular ideas in Judaism should be suppressed. Of course, these were not the only voices within the rabbinate. But over time they came to set the agenda for the European Orthodox world.

### Emigration and Modernity

The mass immigration from Eastern Europe in the nineteenth century helped dynamise the Jewish communities of the West, in particular the United States of America. The New World was particularly hospitable to Reform and Haskalla Judaism. Many of the immigrants were only too eager to throw off the bonds of Jewish practice they associated with the primitive conditions back home. Initially, the communities of the West were seen as the graveyards of Jewish life. Yet surprisingly, other factors have led to a significant revival despite the ongoing trend of assimilation.

In effect the theological challenges of the nineteenth century affected Judaism in very similar ways to Christianity. Humanism and Marxism challenged the traditional assumptions about God and society. Darwinism challenged assumptions about creation, and the industrial society challenged old hierarchies. Some Jews tried to come terms with the challenge through reconciliation. Many were swept up and away from their Jewish roots, while others simply refused to recognise a problem and turned inwards.

During the twentieth century, the theological innovations of German Jews such as Buber, Rosenzweig and Cohen or Abraham Joshua Heshel in America had no impact to speak of on the Orthodox world that simply saw no reason to rethink its language of religious discussion. However, it is probably true to say that more Jews abandoned Judaism attracted by the freedom of the open society than because they had no satisfactory modern theology of Judaism.

Modern Jewish life has been affected dramatically by the rise of nationalism and the events of the twentieth century. Nationalism took on the mantle of Christian exclusivity and Jews were now suspect not for their rejection of the dominant religion but because their own religious culture implied an authority above that of the nation state. Combined with the scientific innovations that were usurped to prove racial superiorities, the nineteenth century had seen an increase in anti-Semitism just as Jews were beginning to enjoy the new winds of emancipation.

## The Sepharadi World

Innovations and changes in Judaism over the past 300 years coincided with the eclipse of Islamic power and the slow decline of the Ottoman Empire. Jews living under Islam fared in general better than under Christendom. However, they shared their political and cultural fate. Their religious leadership and community life was unaffected by the cultural upheavals and reformations of the West.

Oriental Sepharadi communities tended to be more homogenous and traditional. Their rabbis held more authority and influence at a time when reform and assimilation were affecting western congregations. They were more kabbalistic in character, a feature that was used as a tool of communal control. The intellectual advances of the West tended to pass them, by except for the few wealthier members who travelled abroad. Of course, those Sepharadi communities who had moved to Europe and America in the aftermath of 1492 developed altogether a different character.

## Zionism

In the early nineteenth century two Eastern European rabbis, Zvi Kalisher and Judah Alkalai, had started a movement called *Chibbat Zion* (the Love of Zion) with the intention of encouraging as many Jews as possible to move to the Land of Israel to re-establish a dynamic community. There were Jews already living there for ideological and religious reasons, in poverty and dependent on charity, the *challuka* (handouts) raised by collectors in Europe. This new mood was meant to be a more positive one, although still religious.

Zionism began as a liberation movement and the vast majority of its founders were secular, with no religious motivation at all. Despite the importance of Zion in Jewish religious life and the constant to and fro of religious Jews to Israel over the centuries, Zionism was essentially a secular movement. This was why the majority of the Eastern European Orthodox Jewish leadership rejected Zionism. Similarly, most Reform movements rejected the notion of a Jewish homeland as a step backwards.

It was the Nazi Holocaust that led to the extermination of most of Eastern Jewry, supported by the conviction that no one in the world would lift a finger to save Jews unless they saved themselves, that convinced Jews of all sorts, almost universally, to adopt Israel as the centre of Jewish life in one way or another. Although most Orthodox Jews had reservations about a secular state, and most Reform Jews preferred to see themselves as citizens of wherever they lived, they have over the years become reconciled to Israel as the national homeland. Of course Jews vary in their political opinions, and it is dangerous and inaccurate to characterise all Jewish as being left or right wing. It is not possible, therefore, to identify one political position with regard to Israel that is shared by all Jews. What can be said is that Jews can be categorised by the degree of their commitment to their religious tradition.

Nevertheless, Israel has had a profound impact on Jewish religious life. For the first time in 2,000 years, Jewish Law has been applied to every aspect of a viable state. The halachic system had always been dynamic and productive. Each generation produced its own experts who engaged with each other through a process known as Responsa, or in Hebrew *She'elot Uteshuvot* (Questions and Answers). These were written, distributed and discussed amongst experts acknowledged for their mastery of traditional sources. Often a consensus was reached or an agreement to differ. Now new areas of social, political and industrial law have been rejuvenated. Two legal systems coexist In Israel today: the state combination of Turkish, Mandate and Jewish law runs parallel with a complete system of Jewish halachic law. The new universities are powerhouses of Jewish scholarship and research. Similarly, on a philosophical and theological level, there has been a significant increase in creativity. Of course the awesome catastrophe of the Holocaust has affected Jewish theological discussion, but so too has the idea of Israel and redemption.

Jewish theology today manifests similar tensions to those in other religions between the academic and the fundamentalist.

# Chapter 4

# The Jewish Year

## THE PRACTICE OF JUDAISM TODAY

I have intentionally started describing Judaism as it is lived today with practice rather than theology. This is first and foremost because the conventional term 'religion' is not entirely appropriate. Religion can mean simply 'faith'; but Judaism, in common with Islam, is so much more than a faith. It really focuses on every aspect of the way one lives. It is this that defines Judaism, much more than a system of beliefs. Amongst the communities of committed Jews it is practice that unites them more than theology. The practice itself conforms for the most part to a clearly set out and definable constitution called the Halacha. The word is sometimes translated as 'law', but it is much wider than the way we use the word 'law' today.

Most Jewish practices can be traced back to the Talmud and from there back to the Five Books of Moses, the Torah. Those that cannot are in the main, apart from major rabbinic innovations, customs and accretions over the past 2,000 years and do indeed often vary from community to community.

The degree of divergence amongst those who see themselves as bound by Halacha, the traditional system, is really quite marginal. As between the Sepharadim and the Ashkenazim, they are confined to issues such as eating rice at Passover, differences in the pronunciation of Hebrew, and stylistic variations in liturgy. Between different groups of Chassidim, the issues are also pronunciation, dress codes, specific anniversaries of different masters, and times of services. Chassidic men go to the *mikvah*, the ritual bath, to start off every day on a spiritual level, but this not generally followed outside the Chassidic world. In general, however, a practising Jew will recognise most aspects of the life of another practising Jew no matter where in the world he or she comes from, or the extent to which he or she may adhere to all of the traditions or only to some.

## THE CALENDAR

The Jewish year differs in many significant ways from the usual calendar used around the world today. The calendar takes its starting point as the creation of the world, fixed by the rabbis in the fourth century as some 5,764 years ago. Its yearly calculation is a combination of the solar and the lunar cycles.

There are twelve months in a Jewish year whose names are mainly post-biblical. They are now known as, starting in the spring, *Nissan*, followed by *Iyar, Sivan, Tammuz, Av, Ellul, Tishrei, Cheshvan, Kislev, Tevet, Shevat* and *Adar*. They vary in length from 29 to 30 days. The lunar element guarantees that the festivals will always fall in their appropriate season. An extra month, *Adar Sheni* (The Second Adar) is added every so often to keep the months in alignment with the 365-day solar cycle. Theoretically, Nissan ought to be the start of the New Year. This is the implication of the original biblical calendar and the later calendar that went according to the reign of kings. Nowadays the start of the seventh month, Tishrei, is called Rosh Hashanna (the New Year) and the years change then.

The Jewish year is broken down into its most regular component of seven days by the Shabbat, then each month by *Rosh Chodesh*, and then by the seasonal, and finally by the annual festivals.

## Shabbat

Although Shabbat is the first spiritual idea mentioned in the Bible in the second chapter of Genesis, it was not legislated for until the Sinai revelation. The first biblical commandment given to the Children of Israel (as opposed to the Fathers) was the Passover that celebrated the Exodus. Wherever the Torah lists, as it does on several occasions, the festivals, it always starts with Shabbat. Indeed the word 'Shabbat' is used in the Bible for festivals in general as well as for the seventh day. Shabbat is the only festival mentioned in the Ten Commandments, and it is placed within the section that deals with laws relating humanity to God, rather than interhuman legislation. It becomes emblematic of the idea that certain days are devoted to God rather than to conventional society.

The festivals are unique in that they are given with reasons, unlike most of the other biblical laws. In Genesis the seventh day is described as the day on which God rested, but more importantly as the day that He dedicated to Himself by completing the creative process by adding this extra way of being creative, namely through spirituality. In Exodus chapter 20 the Shabbat is explained as commemorating the creation, but in Deuteronomy chapter 5 it is explained in terms of celebrating freedom from slavery. Both ideas are interrelated. Shabbat celebrates the ability to free oneself from total dependence on normal workday or human-dictated activity by creating a different atmosphere once a week.

The Torah associates Shabbat with not doing creative physical work. All building work for the Tabernacle stopped on Shabbat. But the Torah also specifically forbids using fire and 'leaving the area where one lives'. It is from these three ideas that the Shabbat has developed into a day not just of cessation of labour but one in which one tries to create a different atmosphere. Negatively, this has come to mean not relating to society, its mechanisms and entertainments, not switching on electricity, the modern equivalent of 'fire', in the same way one does during the week and preparing food beforehand.

Positively, it means a day devoted to family and community, to prayer, study and celebration where eating together as a family and inviting others to join in, place the emphasis on home as much if not more than on synagogue.

The Shabbat begins an hour before sunset on a Friday and continues until dark (the appearance of three average stars) on the Saturday night. It is initiated by lighting candles in the home and by a service in the synagogue. It was the Safed Kabbalists of the seventeenth century who introduced additional psalms and songs, called *Kabbalat Shabbat* (receiving Shabbat), to welcome in the Shabbat, and these have become universally accepted as an introduction to the Friday evening service. They prepare for the transition from one state to another through meditation and song.

### The Three Meals
At home the household prepares for the first of three Shabbat meals. Husbands bless their wives and parents bless their children. There are songs and poems that welcome in the Shabbat, but the central feature is the dedication of the Shabbat over a cup of wine, *kiddush*. Wine and food play an essential part in every celebratory Jewish meal. Wine adds the element of spiritual festivity and food represents the physical world. The traditions of the meal were established formally in Roman times and based on a Roman banquet, underlining the priority of the home as the centre of Jewish celebration.

After the wine one washes hands before 'breaking bread'. This has to be done with a cup or special vessel for pouring out water. In Temple times one could not eat the tithes unless one was ritually prepared, a process which involved washing, and this idea together with basic hygiene was developed by rabbinic law into the requirement to wash before eating bread. The water is poured onto each hand twice or three times, according to different customs. Visitors will notice that rings, or indeed any other removable barrier to the water, are removed and then one remains silent until one has eaten the bread.

At the back of the table there are two loaves of bread that were covered during Kiddush. A blessing is made called the *motzi*, from the Hebrew wording that thanks God for 'bringing bread from the earth'. The bread is broken or cut and passed around and the meal is under way. At different moments songs may be sung, usually medieval poems in praise of God and Shabbat. There will be 'words of Torah', some explanation of the week's Torah reading and this might be followed by a discussion.

At the end of the meal there is a custom that some observe of washing one's fingertips, *mayim acharonim* (final waters). This comes from a time when one ate with one's fingers and needed to remove the grease and salt. The meal ends with an extended grace-after-meals whose text goes back at least to the Talmud. After the opening invitation to everyone present to join in, the grace is sung or simply said quietly.

The main elements of this meal procedure will be repeated the following midday and at a modified third meal before the end of the Shabbat.

*The Shabbat Synagogue Service*

The Shabbat morning service is longer than on a weekday. It starts with a morning *shacharit* prayer and includes reading a significant section of the Torah. This weekly section of the Torah is called a *Parsha* or a *Sedra*. This is followed by a *Haftara*, a reading from the prophets that is relevant to the Torah reading. Finally, there is an additional service called *musaf*. In many congregations there is a break either to study or for the rabbi to preach.

The combination of prayer and study is an essential feature of festive celebrations. Together with meals, they characterise the positive nature of Shabbat as opposed to the negative restrictions on work and mundane activity. After the service the second meal of Shabbat is held with a similar format to the Friday evening meal.

The afternoon service also has readings from the Torah, but here it is simply the first part of the coming week's portion. The service is followed by studying parts of the Mishna and by the third meal, the *seudat shlishit*. Then after the evening service Shabbat ends. However, there is an additional ceremony of *havdala*, 'dividing' the sacred and the profane. Once again wine is the central part of the ceremony, but fire, whose use was temporarily suspended over Shabbat, and spices are combined to 'compensate' for the loss of the special day.

In Chassidic circles the *melaveh malka* ceremony, literally 'following the queen', is a Saturday night festive meal that extends the atmosphere of Shabbat beyond the letter of the law and is a further opportunity for study, song and spiritual celebration. After the evening service the Chassidim go home to eat and then around midnight gather at the Rebbe's *tisch*, the Yiddish for 'table'. These gatherings, some modest, others massive, are crucial to the Chassidic way of life, reinforcing group loyalty and providing opportunities for the rebbe to reach his faithful.

*Work on Shabbat*

The Bible specifies that one should not work on Shabbat. But what constitutes work? Work on the construction of the biblical tabernacle stopped for Shabbat. This was the basis for explaining the initial parameters of 'work', the thirty-nine categories of work. But work was defined not just as being creative but also as being a mundane, weekday activity. It was not simply a question of hard work, but rather that one had to try to change one's active patterns of behaviour. So the Shabbat was not a leisure day when one stopped doing one sort of routine, but instead it was an occasion for positively creating a very different and a spiritual atmosphere. Writing or commercial transactions, even if they were not 'technically' work, came under the categories we have described and were forbidden. The criterion was not a personal one. Assuming someone slept all week, to work in a quarry on Shabbat would indeed be a change, but hardly a spiritual one.

Making fire was forbidden not because fire was 'hard work', but because it symbolised industry and activity. For this reason modern Jews do not use electrical appliances on Shabbat because electricity represents the basis of society's commercial and industrial activity and also its culture and values.

Shabbat exists to provide a break from the intrusive patterns of the week. The rabbis went further than the Bible and built a fence around those things that remind one of normal activity by insisting that they are not even touched. This does not mean that one cannot have fire at all. As with food, one simply has to prepare everything before Shabbat comes in.

Modern means of transport are forbidden not just because of the 'creativity' of turning on an engine but also, as with animal transport, because they take one away from concentrating on family and home. The Bible specifies that 'one should not leave one's usual area of habitation on Shabbat' (Exodus 16.22). Shabbat and the home are primary. If one can only get to a synagogue by breaking Shabbat, the halachic position is that it is preferable to pray at home.

In preparation for building the Tabernacle, everyone in the camp of the Israelites was invited to bring goods and material for use in the construction. The command not to bring on Shabbat is the basis of the law not to carry anything outside one's private property on Shabbat. This is defined as the home and the town in which one lives. Originally, if one lived in a walled city, the boundaries were easily defined. As cities expanded the issue of what represented one's town and one's property raised new problems.

The rabbis of the Talmud developed the idea of the *eruv*, literally the 'merger'. The eruv is a way of defining territory, one's town, by having symbolic boundaries. Just as one has to prepare one's food before Shabbat, so too one has to prepare one's area of habitation or the area one wishes to use on Shabbat. Most Jewish communities have an eruv, an unobtrusive wire boundary, which enables traditional Jews to carry from one home to another. Of course, the idea is symbolic, but it is another element in making Shabbat a different day.

All the restrictions that apply to Shabbat also apply to festivals, except for two. One may carry on a festival so as to be able to bring in provisions for one's family, and one may cook food, provided the fire has been prepared beforehand.

## THE THREE PILGRIM FESTIVALS

The three pilgrim festivals, Pesach, Shavuot and Succot (Passover, Pentecost and Tabernacles) are mentioned as a separate category in the Torah when everybody was expected to go up to the Temple in Jerusalem, or wherever the Tabernacle was. Jews from around the Land of Israel and then from around the Diaspora would make pilgrimages to Jerusalem on at least one of these festivals every year. One of the tithes, the ma'aser sheni (second tithe) had to be eaten specifically in the centre during these festivals. These community gatherings were an essential feature of Jewish life in Temple times and opportunities for national conventions. Exile put paid to this, but nowadays many religious Jews try to be in Jerusalem for at least one of the three pilgrim festivals. Each of these festivals has three different levels of significance, national, agricultural and spiritual.

## Pesach (Passover)

Passover is the first festival, historically and chronologically. It celebrates the freedom from slavery in Egypt. Its message is that we are all enslaved in one way or another and true liberation is when we accept a spiritual master rather than a human one.

The 'first' Passover in Egypt had certain specific laws (Exodus 12). Each family had to take a lamb to be sacrificed and its blood would be spread over the doorposts so that God would pass over those houses daubed in blood. The lamb had to be roasted, using no vessels that might need cleaning. The meal was taken in travelling clothes, ready to depart as soon as the word came and nothing could be left over.

From this specific beginning, the Passover was ordained as a permanent festival. Sacrificing the paschal lamb remained obligatory, but it could only be eaten in Jerusalem. After the loss of the Temple, an elaborate meal called the Seder was developed instead.

The overriding feature of the whole Passover festival, which lasts eight days, is the need to remove any trace of leaven, *chametz*, symbolising the bread of affliction of slavery, but also to recall the unleavened bread that the Children of Israel ate as they fled Egypt in too much of hurry to allow the bread time to rise. This need to remove chametz is taken very seriously in traditional households and results in a very thorough 'spring-clean' each year. In a ceremony to 'check and remove' the evening before Passover, the 'search' is still carried out by candlelight with a feather used symbolically to sweep up the crumbs, despite the fact that modern technology makes cleaning with a vacuum cleaner much easier and in better light than in the past.

All chametz must be removed and over Passover no food that has any leavened ingredient, however small, may be eaten. In addition, *matzah*, unleavened bread with absolutely no added ingredient, becomes the staple diet. The laws for making unleavened bread are complex. They involve overseeing the wheat from harvesting, seeing that the water used has not been left uncovered and then making sure that the dough is finely rolled out so that no lumps or pockets exist which would allow fermentation. Finally, the baking has to be done within a short interval before the oven and utensils have to be cleaned before re-use. Although mechanically baked matzahs are universally available, many Jews prefer to use only hand-baked matzahs for the Seder meal.

On the day of Passover the first-born fast to commemorate their deliverance, when the last of the plagues hit Pharaoh and his people by killing their firstborn. Since talmudic times, whenever a person finishes a volume of the

Talmud, he has a celebratory meal. It has now become accepted practice that someone in each community finishes a volume on the eve of Passover so that the celebratory meal overrides the fast.

The festival is introduced as any Shabbat with candles at home and a service in the synagogue, and then the Seder meal is held. This protracted meal is the most complex and heavily symbolic of all the celebratory meals throughout the year. Seder simply means 'order' or 'sequence'.

Its origins are to be found in the Talmud. The essential elements include the presence of three matzahs, unleavened loaves, four cups of wine to celebrate the four terms for salvation from slavery mentioned in the Torah, bitter herbs called *maror*, and symbols of the Passover sacrifice and the festival sacrifice that were part of the Temple service. The paschal lamb's presence remained only symbolically in the roast bone placed at the meal. In deference to the loss of the Temple, the one food not eaten on the Passover night nowadays is roast lamb.

A special obligation was introduced to talk about the Exodus in all its aspects throughout the night. The Talmud introduces the four questions that everyone should ask as a lead into discussion, 'Why is this night different from all other nights?'; moreover, a special *Haggadah* (book of narrative) evolved to be used on the seder night to provide an agenda for the discussions.

Unusual customs were added in order to encourage question and debate. Herbs called *karpas* are dipped into salt water and eaten before the meal. A sweet paste of nuts, wine and apples or dates called *charoset*, to commemorate the mortar used during slave labour, is prepared to be eaten with the bitter herbs. Eggs in salt water, a symbol of life and death, are eaten before the main food is brought to table. A piece of matzah called by its Greek name, *afikoman*, literally the desert, is hidden for children to look for and is the last thing to be eaten at the end. At the Seder everyone reclines as at a Roman banquet and wears the white robes of the High Priest. The whole effect was designed to encourage everyone to participate, to question and to seek answers.

Originally there was one day at the start of the festival and one at the end when the strictures of a Shabbat applied, with the sole exception of preparing food. So long as a fire had been kept burning in advance, one was and is allowed to cook on a festival, whereas one cannot on Shabbat. There were five intermediary days called *Chol HaMoed* (the festive weekdays) during Passover on which essential work can be done. They are regarded as semi-festive and festive clothes are worn and only essential work is done.

### The Second Day of the Festival

The Jewish monthly calendar was originally fixed on the basis of sighting the new moon. Witnesses who had seen it were required to come and give their testimony in Jerusalem or wherever the rabbinic court sat before a new month was declared. In the Babylonian Diaspora, it took time for the news to arrive from Israel as to when the new month was declared. Even in Israel itself sightings of the moon could be delayed and the daily Temple order confused. As a result, the Diaspora kept two days for each festival instead of one. The only exception to this was Rosh Hashanna, the New Year, which was fixed as a two-day festival even in the Land of Israel to ensure that there would be no last minute errors. Although expertise on the calendar during the later days of the Second Commonwealth meant that the calendar was effectively fixed more than 2,000 years ago, there was universal agreement that the Diaspora should retain the two-day strictness. Some argued that once in place, a custom should not be rescinded. The Diaspora had fewer ritual obligations and this was a necessary means of reinforcing identity. Within the traditional world nowadays, those living in Israel keep one day and those outside keep two. So in the Diaspora there are two Seder nights, but in Israel only one.

The last day (or two) of Passover has no specific customs other than the continuing ban on leavened bread. It is the anniversary of the crossing of the Red Sea and in Chassidic circles, in particular, it has symbolic associations with exile. In some groups the rebbe, the head of the community, actually relives the experience by running up and down between singing banks of the faithful to recreate the tensions and the sense of relief aroused by the original experience.

Each of the three pilgrim festivals is associated with a biblical scroll. On Passover it is the *Song of Songs*. This beautiful love poem, attributed to King Solomon, was regarded by Rabbi Akivah as the holiest book of the Bible. Rabbi Akivah argued that it was a parable of the love between God and his faithful. His was a mystical point of view, one that beautifully illustrates the way the rabbis saw the relationship between man and God. It is read on Passover because this is, in a way, the beginning of the 'love affair' between the Jewish people and God.

### The Omer

Pesach also marks the start of the new agricultural year and no new produce from that year could be eaten before the *Omer* (the first sheaf of the first barley harvest) had been dedicated. The process of 'counting the Omer' starts on the second night of Passover. According to the Torah, this involved counting forty-nine days, seven weeks, from the start of the barley harvest leading up to the festival of Pentecost and the wheat harvest. Every day and every week from Passover is counted up until Shavuot, the festival of weeks, known as Pentecost.

This period has become one of mourning. It started at the time of the Bar Cochba Revolution in 132 CE when large numbers of the pupils of Rabbi Akivah died. The Talmud ascribes this to a lack of respect one for the other, but in general the Talmud avoids too much historical association. It prefers to emphasise the spiritual. Yet we know that Akivah supported Bar Cochba and died as a result. Later, the period just after Easter became one of almost constant Christian persecution. Sermons on the passion of Jesus inevitably brought retribution on the Jews. It was not, after all, until Pope John XXIII that the Jews of today were absolved of guilt for the crucifixion. Easter was also the time of the year when the Crusades, bloody and catastrophic for Jews, began their murderous trails through Europe towards the Holy Land. As a result no marriages or other festivities take place during this period. The clean-shaven allow their beards and hair to grow, and nothing new is bought. The only break is on the thirty-third day of the Omer, the anniversary of the great Kabbalist Shimon Bar Yochai, which is marked by a day of festivity and celebration. In particular, his tomb at Meron, in northern Israel, is the centre of great celebration, primarily by the Sepharadi communities with their greater sympathy for the mystical tradition.

## Shavuot (Pentecost)

Shavuot is mentioned in the Torah exclusively as a harvest festival. It is the festival of the First Fruits and the start of the wheat harvest. It is a one-day festival (two in the Diaspora) and in some ways is an adjunct to or a completion of the Passover. It was a counterbalance to pagan harvest festivals. The Torah repeats the phrase 'Do not boil a kid goat in its mother's milk' three times in the context of this festival. We now know this to have been an essential fertility rite at harvest time, going back to Ugarit.

After the destruction of the Temple, Shavuot was given added importance as the anniversary of the covenant between Israel and God on Sinai. Nowadays both ideas play an important part in the way Shavuot is celebrated. Synagogues are festooned with flowers and plants, and a light dairy dish rather than meat is served at the festive meal. All sorts of reasons for this custom have been advanced, but in all probability it has more to do with a summer diet than the most common explanation that after the Sinai revelation and the dietary laws, they could only prepare a milk meal because the meat-cooking utensils would have to be cleansed.

On the first night of Shavuot people gather in synagogues and homes to study all through the night. This relatively recent custom is a sort of re-enactment of the Sinai experience, called *Tikkun Leil Shavuot*, literally 'the order (programme) of the eve of Shavuot'.

The book of the Bible associated with Shavuot is the Book of Ruth. It conveniently brings both themes together. It is set at harvest time and illustrates the way the poor of any persuasion could take advantage of the strict biblical laws of charity that prescribed the opening up one's fields at harvest time to the poor. The book is also an affirmation of commitment to Judaism. Just as Ruth decided to accept a Jewish way of life, so too Shavuot is the occasion for every Jew to reaffirm his or her commitment.

## Succot (Tabernacles)

After Shavuot, the next festivals chronologically are Rosh Hashanna, the New Year, and Yom Kippur, the Day of Atonement. Succot, Tabernacles, comes after Yom Kippur in the year. However, the Torah always puts the three pilgrim festivals together.

Succot is the third and last of the harvest festivals. It comes in the autumn when agricultural society has completed its cycle and all the produce has been gathered in. It is also the moment at which, in the northern hemisphere, nature turns from fruitfulness to 'hibernation'. Its national significance is given as its commemoration of the period of wandering in the desert, with only temporary shelter, relying on divine protection. The *Succah* symbolises this.

### The Succah

The Succah, a temporary booth according to the Talmud, which everyone had to live in during the festival, was a common structure in an agricultural society. Isaiah refers to the loneliness of a Succah, the watchman's booth, as he protects vineyards or fields during the summer heat. It was intended to underline the fragility of life and human dependence on God.

The Talmud defines a Succah by its roof, made of anything grown from the ground that is now detached from it. It must have two and a half walls and be big enough to shelter most of an individual. On the other hand, it should not be so high that one does not notice the *sechach* (roof). Although the Talmud envisions people using the Succah as home during the festival, for eating, sleeping and relaxing in, it allows them to 'escape' in the event of inclement weather conditions.

### The Four Plants

The second feature of the festival is the *arba'a minim*, the four kinds (of plants). The Bible (Leviticus 23.40) mentions taking 'the fruit of a pleasant tree, date palms, a branch of a thick tree and of willows of the brook.' Only the willow and the date palm are specified, the other two, citron and myrtle, are good examples of the oral tradition clarifying the written. They were taken and bound together and used in processions in the Temple. Nowadays they are waved during a special selection of joyful psalms, *hallel*, added into the daily festive service and they are taken in procession around the synagogue.

They are particularly dependent on rain for survival. Some need irrigation; others find their source of water through their deep roots. These four plants symbolised the role of nature in its widest sense. The act of holding and touching natural objects that normally are taken for granted reinforced the interconnection between God, humanity and nature. At a mystical level the four plants represent human characteristics and the different channels of divine intervention in human affairs.

*Praying for Rain*

Rain played such a crucial part in Middle Eastern life then as now, that it gave rise to a whole slew of fasts and ceremonies. One of them that has been revived is the custom dating back to the prophets when priests led 'rejoicing around the Well House'. During the five intermediary days of the Festival there were processions around the Temple well and poured out water, *Nisuch HaMayim*, as part of the ceremonies asking God for rain. Then in the evenings public parties were held, lit up by huge bonfires. Nowadays on each night of the intermediary days, yeshivas, the equivalent of theological colleges, run festivities with music and dance through the night.

The last of the intermediary days is called *Hoshanna Rabba*, the great salvation. It is a post-biblical celebration that completed the rain processions around the Temple. It has become a tradition now to stay up all night studying Torah, but in the morning the services culminate with everyone in the community taking three willow branches and beating them on the steps of the synagogue. In all probability this was to do with rain, but it has now come to symbolise sweeping away one's misdemeanours. The salvation referred to here is not a theological one but again has to do with rain and physical survival.

*Shemini Atzeret and Simchat Torah*

The final day or days of Succot are called *Shemini Atzeret* (the congregation of the eighth day) and in the Diaspora the following day is *Simchat Torah* (the rejoicing of the law). On Shemini Atzeret the prayers asking for rain (which were suspended over the summer from Pesach) are reintroduced into the daily service. At this stage, the themes of nature and rain, so pervasive throughout the festival hitherto and the Succah, give way to a totally different atmosphere.

The Bible emphasises 'joy' during the festivals (Leviticus 23) in general, and specifically it records the command twice for Succoth. But how did it come about that the last day became particularly devoted to what one might call 'excessive joy'?

Studying Torah, as the essential bond that kept communities together and ensured their survival, increased in significance. Reading the Torah in public had become frequent since Ezra's time. It was later read on Mondays and Thursdays when the outlying populace would come into towns for the main markets. Then the Torah was read in public on Shabbat and festivals. Initially small sections were read in the original Hebrew and then translated into the vernacular Aramaic and read sequentially. Different customs began to emerge; some communities read through the Torah every seven years, others three and some one. By the end of the talmudic era, the annual cycle had gained all but universal acceptance.

Simchat Torah, the last day of Succot, was fixed as the moment at which the past annual cycle ended and the new one began. In Israel this coincides with Shemini Atzeret, but in the Diaspora it stands independently on the second of the last two days of the festival. In the synagogue there are songs and dancing, and wine and cakes are offered around. From the eldest and wisest down, the Torah and its unique role in linking Jews to God is celebrated ecstatically (the more reticent Anglo-Jewish communities tend to play things down a little). It was on Simchat Torah that the seventeenth-century diarist Samuel Pepys visited the Spanish and Portuguese synagogue Bevis Marks in London and described the Jewish service as one of sacrilegious chaos.

## THE DAYS OF AWE

### Rosh Hashanna (New Year)

Two important festivals have come to be regarded as the holiest days of the Jewish calendar. In the Bible Rosh Hashanna is called *Yom HaZikaron*, the day of remembering, or *Yom Teruah*, the day when the *Shofar* (the ram's horn) is blown. It is in the Mishna that we come across the distinction between the new year for months and the new year for years. Somewhere between the Torah and the Mishna the name Rosh Hashanna was applied and its symbolical association with the creation of the world established. Rosh Hashanna prepares for the Day of Atonement, Yom Kippur, ten days later and the intervening days have come to be known as the ten days of repentance.

### *The Shofar*

Rosh Hashanna is a two-day festival, even in Israel. As the result of an error in Temple times, which led to the priests performing the festival service at the wrong time, Rosh Hashanna became a two-day festival. In Temple times the shofar was the essential feature, but rabbinic innovation led to the ban on blowing the shofar if Rosh Hashanna fell on a Shabbat.

Maimonides suggests that the sound of the Shofar was designed both to recall our forefathers' quest to engage with God, and to wake us up from our spiritual slumber so that we might re-establish contact with God, given the human tendency to allow standards and disciplines to slide.

The Shofar is sounded a hundred times during the course of the synagogue service and it has three different notes. These were the sounds used in the wilderness as a way of communicating with everyone. The *tekia* was the sound used to announce a meeting; the *teruah* was the sound of alarm, and the *shevarim* was the sound of sadness and mourning. These notes are sounded separately and in combination.

The liturgy that evolved was built around the Shofar sounds. There are three themes, of 'kingship', 'remembering', and 'Shofar'. The Shofar reminds everyone of the obligation to accept divine authority. It also calls on God to remember his people. The aim of the day is to assert the need to repent and then to give time before the Day of Atonement to effect change. Special penitential poems, most of them medieval, were later introduced and said every morning from the week before Rosh Hashanna until Yom Kippur. In Sepharadi communities they are said throughout the preceding month of Ellul when all communities sound the Shofar once at the end of the weekday morning service.

In common with other festivals, Rosh Hashanna is a day when no work is done other than the preparation of food provided the means have been prepared in advance.

## Yom Kippur (The Day of Atonement)

The Day of Atonement is described in the Torah as the day when 'you shall afflict your souls' (Leviticus 23.27). This was understood by the Oral law to mean fasting. It is the only fast day prescribed in the Torah. The Temple ceremony was a unique one with two goats atoning for the community, one of which became the 'scapegoat' that was sent out into the desert bearing the sins of the community. This was the only occasion when the High Priest, dressed in white, pronounced the true name of God. Otherwise synonyms were used.

The Mishna records that after the brief ceremony was over, the community left the Temple in high spirits, convinced of God's benevolence. Young men and women dressed in white went dancing in vineyards and selected marriage partners. This is a far cry from the very solemn atmosphere that prevails nowadays, when many stay the whole day in the synagogue saying penitential prayers and participating in a service that over the past thousand years has given poetic expression to the almost continuous crisis of Jewish life in exile. The language of metaphor is constantly used to create an image of mankind being judged and decisions about the quality of human lives being taken on this day and being 'written in the book of life and death'.

### Kol Nidrei

The evening service starts with *kol nidrei* (all vows). This is a declaration in which those present ask for forgiveness of vows taken on matters to do with God (in Jewish law any vow taken to do with other humans can only be annulled with their agreement or via a court judgement). There remain different variations of this ancient prayer; some apply it to the past year, and others to the future. Either way the declaration underlines the fact that the Day of Atonement only applies to matters between humans and God. This is a way of 'clearing the decks' of any unfulfilled commitments before starting to reassess oneself in relation to God. If one has any outstanding debts or issues with other human beings, these need to be settled before one begins the process of atonement.

The pattern of services is similar to that of any festive day except that the custom has developed to spend much more time in the synagogue. There are no festive meals to go home to (although the final meal before the fast is indeed treated festively). An additional service, unique to Yom Kippur, is the last service of the day, called *neilah*, literally the closing of the gates, the final opportunity to intercede with our heavenly Judge. This is also when everyone focuses on the hopes for a good coming year. If the metaphor of Pesach is to imagine what it is like to be free, the metaphor of Yom Kippur is to imagine what it is like to be judged. The long history of Jewish suffering has had a profound effect on this day.

Many beautiful but complex medieval poems called *piyutim* have been added over the years. The fate of the Jewish people over the centuries led to this being a day when Jews would beseech their Maker to protect them and their families from the suffering that often befell them. It is true to say that the long history of exile dictates the heavy, mournful atmosphere that now permeates the day.

### Rosh Chodesh (New Moon)

The only other 'festival' mentioned in the Torah is the new moon, *Rosh Chodesh*. Outside the Temple there were no ceremonies or restrictions attached to it. Sometimes it would last for one day, sometimes for two. Additional prayers are added both to the daily services and to the grace after meals. In medieval times the new moon was regarded as an additional female day of rest, when women were encouraged to celebrate with some hard-earned leisure. Nowadays it is recognised only through additional prayers.

## POST-BIBLICAL FESTIVALS

### Purim

The first 'post-biblical' festival, Purim, is mentioned in the Book of Esther. It records an attempt by Haman, a Persian power-broker, to have the Jews of the Empire destroyed (about 2,500 years ago) and the way in which his plans were thwarted.

Purim is the only significant festival of Diaspora origin. Because of its post-biblical origin the restrictions on work and the use of fire forbidden at biblical festivals do not apply. It has become the nearest Judaism has to carnival and usually takes place in March.

The story is one of archetypal anti-Semitism that characterises the position of the Jew in the Diaspora as 'the other'. The Bible has a specific law about the tribe of Amalek (Exodus 17.8; Deuteronomy 25.17), which attacked the rear of the Children of Israel without provocation as they emerged from Egypt. Amalek is the archetypal enemy for no apparent reason. Whereas the seven Canaanite tribes might have had good cause to fight the invading Children of Israel, Amalek did not. In the generation of the Judge Samuel, Aggag was the Amalekite King whom Saul was commanded to destroy. Haman is described as a descendant of Aggag.

The good fortune of there being a Jewish queen at the time helped, together with Mordecai's intervention, to avert the decree and despair was turned to joy. As result Mordecai and Esther instituted the custom of cele-brations, feasts and gifts both to the poor and to friends that have been incorporated into Jewish law.

Over the years celebrations became more intense. The Talmud talks about the need to be so happy (possibly drunk) that you cannot tell the difference between 'cursed is Mordecai and blessed is Haman'. Somewhere in the post-talmudic world the custom of getting dressed up in disguise emerged. The rationale for this was that the story of Esther is one of disguise. The name of God is not mentioned in the book, and yet divine intervention seems every-where. Things are not as they seem. Of course, the sad history of Jewish persecution added serious days to the calendar, but it also meant that those few occasions for merriment that existed were seized upon and savoured.

The central ceremony is the public reading of the Book of Esther with noise and catcalls greeting the name of Haman whenever it is mentioned. A major festive meal with charades and songs is held in the afternoon of Purim itself and at least two presents of two different kinds of food have to be sent to friends, in addition to larger than normal charitable gifts to the poor.

The day before Purim is a fast, the Fast of Esther, which imitates the fast she herself performed before she went into the king to beg for the lives of the Jewish people.

## Chanukah

The second post-biblical festival is Chanukah, which falls in December. It records the struggle between the Maccabees and the Syrian Greeks that flared up after the Seleucid king Antiochus IV tried to impose pagan religion on the Jews in the third century BCE. Matthathius, a rural priest, initiated the revolt that was led by his son Judah (Judah the Hammerer, hence the title Maccabee). He managed, through a series of guerrilla successes, to regain control of the Temple and much of the Jewish territory. He was indirectly helped by internal struggles in the Seleucid Empire.

Despite his victories Judah failed to remove the Syrian garrison from Jerusalem. Over time the family succeeded in re-establishing Jewish hege-mony and independence. Sadly, the Maccabee dynasty declined both in influence and in its commitment to Judaism, culminating in the Herodian monarchy. As a result, the rabbis of the Talmud tried to minimise the Maccabean involvement and Judah is not mentioned in the Talmud.

What did become the focal point of religious celebration was the story that when the Temple was re-dedicated in 165 BCE, there was only enough oil to last to keep the eternal light in the *menorah* (candelabrum) burning for one day. But it was eight days before the new supply could arrive. The oil lasted and this is the miracle that the eight days of Chanukah record. It is no co-incidence that Solomon's dedication of the first Temple also lasted for eight days. The history of the Maccabees is recorded in the Books of the Maccabees, but these were excluded from the biblical canon.

The Talmud records the custom of lighting lights for eight days. Hillel's insistence on starting with one and adding a light a day, rising to eight, became the accepted custom. The word menorah initially applied only to the seven-branched candelabrum in the Temple. In modern Hebrew, the eight-branched Chanukah version is called the *Chanukia*. Chanukah, like Purim, is not festival on which work and mundane activity is forbidden. Medieval customs included playing with spinning tops, called dreidels (the Yiddish name betrays its origin), and frying cakes in oil (doughnuts) to record the centrality of oil in the celebrations.

## POST-BIBLICAL FASTS

The Book of Zechariah records a series of fasts that were introduced in the wake of the destruction of the first Temple in 586 BCE. The most significant is the ninth of Av, which records the destruction of the Temple. This is the only fast-day that imitates the Day of Atonement by starting at sundown and lasting for twenty-five hours. After the second Temple was destroyed in 70 CE, it too was commemorated on this day. The Book of Lamentations, attributed to the prophet Jeremiah, recording the destruction of Jerusalem is read and medieval poems of mourning called *kinot* are read. Normal chairs are abandoned for low mourning-stools and some synagogues use candlelight. Within the Orthodox community this day is also accepted as a day of mourning for the Holocaust (Israel's establishment of a Holocaust day in May notwithstanding).

There is a sequence of other fasts that lead up to the ninth of Av. In the winter the tenth of Tevet is when the sieges of Jerusalem began. The seventeenth of Tammuz records the destruction of the walls of Jerusalem, and the three weeks between this date and the ninth of Av are traditionally kept as a period of mourning in which weddings and festivities do not take place.

The fast of Gedalia falls on the day after the New Year, Rosh Hashanna. Gedalia was the governor of Judea left in charge by the Babylonians after the destruction in 586 BCE. He was assassinated and the remnants of the Jews fled to Egypt. The fast's significance lies in the fact that this was the only time since the original settlement when no Jews at all were left in Israel. The fast of Gedalia is also part of the ten days of penitence that stretch from Rosh Hashanna to Yom Kippur. This sombre period is not referred to in the Bible and so counts as a post-biblical innovation.

Two other fasts have entered the calendar, the fast of Esther and the fast of the Firstborn on the day before Passover. In medieval times a voluntary series of fasts called the *behab* fasts emerged. The name is a combination of the letters of the Hebrew alphabet that stand for Monday, Thursday and Monday. Following Succot and Pesach, these particular days were adopted as a sort of penance for excess, but nowadays they are only maintained by the very strict. They mirror a medieval religious tendency towards self-denial that borrows from Christian conventions and also reflects the frame of mind of much of medieval Jewry.

## ISRAEL'S INDEPENDENCE DAY, YOM HA ATSMAUT

Israel's Independence Day is celebrated with additional thanksgiving prayers and a special 'order of service'. Most of the very Orthodox Charedi world does not accept decisions taken by the secular Israeli *Knesset* (parliament) as having any religious validity. They believe that only the Messiah can herald a formal return to Zion and they do not see Zionism as a way of achieving Jewish freedom from exile. Only the religious nationalists and the modern or middle Orthodox treat Israel's Independence day as a religious occasion for celebration.

Finally, individual Chassidic communities have introduced their own specific festive days, which are associated with specific events in the lives of their leaders. But the majority of Jews do not celebrate these today.

# Chapter 5

# The Jewish Day

## PRAYER, SERVICES AND SYNAGOGUE

According to the codes of Jewish Law the first thing one does on waking up is to thank God for being alive and conscious, even before leaving one's bed. Then one washes one's hands and prepares to meet the day. The day starts with prayer.

Maimonides says that the Bible requires one to pray to God in any way, any language and any form, and at any time a person feels moved to do so. He suggests that after the Babylonian Exile Jews lost the facility to express themselves not only in Hebrew but in general, and prayers were formulated as a menu for people to choose from in order to express their emotional and spiritual needs. In the Temple itself there were no prayers, except when the High Priest entered the Holy of Holies to ask forgiveness for himself, his family, the priesthood and Israel. The Hebrew word for prayer, *TeFiLLa*, is not derived from the word 'to ask' as in English, but from the words to 'express' or to 'judge' oneself.

### The Shema

There is another Torah obligation, to recite the *Shema*, the three paragraphs from Deuteronomy chapter 6 verses 4–9, chapter 11 verses 13–21, and Numbers chapter 15 verses 37–41. It starts with probably the single most important phrase in Judaism: 'Hear (Shema) Israel, YHVH is our God, YHVH is One.' This is the nearest Judaism gets to a confession of faith. The verse continues, 'And you shall love the Lord your God with all your heart.' This has to be recited in the morning and in the evening. Originally it was quite independent of prayer and was recited during Temple times. Later it was incorporated within the morning and evening prayer services. The rabbis added blessings before and after the Shema that came to be known as the Blessings of the Shema. Nowadays the Shema itself is repeated before going to sleep, as well as in the morning and evening prayers.

### The Amida

After the destruction of the Temple, the rabbis of Yavneh introduced daily prayer to replace the sacrifices as community expressions of religion to supplement private practice. They mirrored the Temple service and incorporated prayers that had already been in use from previous generations.

Although they are rabbinic obligations (and can be said anywhere), they were intended to be recited in the presence of at least ten adult men, the *Minyan*, literally the 'number', so as to perpetuate the notion of community. The number 'ten' derives from the biblical definition of a minimum 'community'.

Prayers could be said in any language, but the decision to fix them in Hebrew, and to a lesser extent Aramaic, was calculated to act as a cohesive factor linking Jews across the various cultural boundaries they lived in. In the second century the word 'prayer' in a halachic context came to apply quite specifically to the eighteen blessings, *Shemona Esreh*, also known as the *Amida*, for it is, as the word implies, a prayer said standing.

The prayers that replaced the two daily temple sacrifices are called *Shacharit* (morning); *Mincha* (afternoon); and a third, *Maariv* (evening) (originally optional) was added. On those occasions when an extra festive sacrifice would have been offered in the Temple, the *musaf*, an additional prayer, extends the morning service. Services are 'led' by a representative of the community who does not need to be a priest or rabbi. It was in medieval Spain that the role of *Chazan*, originally an official of the synagogue, became that of Cantor, a layman with a pleasant voice whose function was to sing prayers in such a way as to inspire the community. In many Orthodox communities nowadays the role of Chazan as opposed to 'leader' has been abandoned, except perhaps on the Days of Awe.

## Reading the Torah

Another important feature of services is *Keriat HaTorah*, reading from the Torah. This is far older than formal prayer and is in fact a separate command of biblical origin. Then it was specified only as part of the Jubilee celebrations. Later it became a regular feature.

The earliest custom of reading parts of the Torah in public on market days is reflected in the current custom of reading the first part of each week's Sabbath portion on the Monday and Thursday morning services. The Torah is read on Shabbat and on every festival, as well as on Shabbat and Yom Kippur afternoons. Individuals do not have to read the Torah when praying alone (but they may read it any time they want to for study).

A scroll of the Torah contains the first five books of the scriptures, known as the Five Books of Moses, written in black ink on parchment with a quill, by a scribe known as a *Sofer*. The scribe is often called a Sofer STAM (STAM stands for Sefer Torah, Tefillin, phylacteries and *Mezuzah*, the scroll placed on doors of Jewish homes to indicate their dedication to the Torah). All public readings from the Torah have to be from a scroll written in this way. Otherwise, for study or other uses a printed version called the *Chumash* (literally 'The Five' as in Five Books of Moses) is used. Other books of the Bible are often also written on parchment scrolls, particularly those read on festivals, but only the scroll of the Book of Esther must be written this way.

The services the rabbis initiated consisted of these three major elements, the Shema, the Amida and, when relevant, a reading from the Torah. Later on additional blessings that the Talmud expects individuals to say privately at home when they wake up were added, plus extracts from the Mishna and a collection of Psalms to help create a mood of devotion before getting to the Shema. Other prayers and confessionals were added after the Amida as a way of slowly winding down after the climax of the essential prayer.

## The Synagogue

Originally the Babylonian exile gave rise to the Beth Midrash, simply a study house which also doubled as a community centre. Later it became known as the *Beth HaKnesset* (the House of Gathering). This was also where the Torah was recited. As communal prayers were introduced they too were said there.

There is debate in the Talmud as to whether it is better to pray where one studies or go to join the community in the synagogues. The Orthodox tradition of today usually combines the two and more study is done throughout the day than prayer. But in communities where there is little study, the synagogue becomes the focal point of religious life.

In Chassidic circles the prayer/study house is called the *Shtiebel*, little house in Yiddish, and was, and often is, no more than a room in a house. All that is needed is an *Aron*, a container or 'Ark' in which the scrolls of the Torah are kept, a *Bima*, platform or table, centrally placed, from which the Torah is read, and a simple lectern in front of the Ark from where the prayers are led. Sometimes the latter two are combined. But other than facing towards Jerusalem, there are no other requirements.

The one feature that Muslim and Jewish places of prayer share in contrast to Christianity is that no human representation is allowed. Surprisingly, given the legal framework for passing on the Jewish religious tradition, one might have expected there to be a serious body of law relating to the structure of the synagogue. In practice there is very little. There have been no wars in Judaism over the positioning of altars or the architectural layout of the buildings. But there are laws concerned with how to behave inside a synagogue, when it can be sold and where it figures in the list of priorities within a community.

## Women in the Synagogue

The development of the synagogue, over 2,000 years ago, came at a time when women were not required to play a leading role outside the home. Since the home was the essential feature of Jewish religious life, the idea of giving women a role in public was not even considered. The obligations of home and family were regarded as overriding. As the Psalmist says (Psalms 45.14), 'A king's daughter's glory is inside.'

Women did indeed come up to the Temple and offer sacrifices. The Talmud in *Succah* records that on the Festival of Succot the Temple was so crowded that a special platform was built for women so that they would not be humiliated in the crush of bodies. Originally, synagogues were established in commercial centres as meeting places and, as a result, no provision was made for women. Women were freed from public obligations and those related to time. Consequently, attendance at the synagogue was optional. This is why women in traditional communities had no role in the public services and why later on separate seating was arranged for them.

This is one of the areas that differentiates Orthodox Judaism from Reform. Reform and most Conservative congregations have abandoned all ritual differences between the sexes and so no division between the sections for males and females will be found. Reform also tends to introduce features borrowed from Christianity, such as the organ, and to have instrumental accompaniment at services.

## The Tsitsit and Talit

Although different Jewish communities throughout the world have their own dress codes and customs, all traditional Jews wear the *Arba Kanfot*, the four-cornered garment with its fringes, called *Tsitsit*, as mentioned in the Torah (Numbers 15.37). Originally this referred to fringes on the four-cornered garment, namely the tunic or toga that everyone wore. These little knots and tassels on the corners of one's clothes were designed as a reminder of one's religious obligations. As fashions changed, a special garment thrown over one's head and neck, falling down like a priest's tunic, was designed to be worn over or under one's regular garments with the fringes inside or out according to custom. These are now part of the tradition and are put on as one dresses, with the appropriate blessing.

The *Talit* is worn in the synagogue or for prayers. In some communities only married men wear it. The Talit is a 'prayer shawl' with a Tsitsit on it; it was only used in synagogues and to maintain the tradition of wearing a four-cornered garment when it was no longer the current mode of dress. Nowadays it has been added to the armoury of ritual, even though technically the simpler garment suffices. But its function in prayer is to enable one to 'wrap oneself up' in a private place and concentrate.

## The Tefillin (Phylacteries)

The *Tefillin* draw on the biblical source in Deuteronomy (6.4–9) to bind the words of God to one's heart and mind. Black leather boxes containing four sections of the Torah are written on parchment and rolled separately for the hand version (placed on the bicep opposite the heart) and together in the head version, placed at the top of the forehead against the brain. The boxes are called *batim* (houses). They are held in position by black leather straps, called *retsuot*. One puts them on to dedicate the emotional and the intellectual human to God. Having originally been worn all day, nowadays Tefillin are only worn during weekday morning service (except on the ninth of Av when they are worn at Mincha).

The four sections of the Torah come from the beginning and from the middle of Exodus chapter 13, and the first two paragraphs of the Shema. There is disagreement as to the precise order of these sections and as a result mainstream Judaism follows the opinion of the medieval authority Rashi. Chassidim have taken upon themselves to wear a second pair each day with the dissenting version of Rabbeynu Tam. It is only the order not the content that differs.

A much later innovation is the headgear known variously as *cappel*, *yarmulke* or *kippa* in Israel. Probably everyone, except for slaves, covered their head in the hot Middle East. The Bible only specifies headgear for the priesthood. But as fashions changed, it became traditional for both for men and women to cover their heads either with a hat or a scarf. Perhaps the Graeco-Roman fashion of not covering the head was something that the Jews of the time wanted to distance themselves from.

At some stage in medieval times special indoor headgear developed and, although not mentioned in the Talmud, the small hat that symbolises God's presence became a universal custom. As Jews moved out into the wider world and followed local dress codes, the cappel's use was limited to rituals, such as during prayer, eating or blessings. Nowadays in more Orthodox communities the black hat has become the universal uniform, even for North African Sepharadim who used to glory in Arab dress. Nevertheless, the cappel is usually worn underneath a hat and is only exposed at home or in the study halls. Its many varieties of colour and shape are an easy way of identifying the wearer's loyalties in the range of Jewish practices.

## BLESSINGS

The Hebrew word for 'blessing', *BeRaCHa*, is derived from the words that mean 'to worship by bending one's knee' or 'to care for a child'. The implication is that a blessing is either a statement of worship or one that expresses care and concern. Whenever a parent blesses a child or a person 'blesses' God, this is an expression of care and it can also be an act of worship.

### Grace after Meals

The Bible records the need to eat and be satisfied and to thank God (Deuteronomy 8.10). This is the origin of the grace-after-meals that is obligatory for everyone. As with other pleasures, one blesses God before enjoying food. But after every meal or food there is a grace-after-meals. It is longest after bread, with three extended blessings, but there are two shorter 'after blessings' for other foods. These are private obligations, but when three people eat a main meal together (as defined by having bread) they invite each other to say grace in a ceremony called *zimun* (invitation). From this principle of being satisfied and thanking God developed the idea that one should engage with God before any activity and before and after any pleasure.

The Talmud goes in great detail into these blessings that extend from eating and drinking to seeing natural phenomena, experiencing unusual events, and hearing good or bad news. Every aspect of life is sanctified. There is a talmudic tradition that a person should make 100 blessings every day. The biblical statement that Jews are a nation of priests is designed to underline the idea that everyone has the capacity for holiness and should strive to lead a holy life. Judaism does not see holiness in terms of withdrawing from life but rather actively participating and adding a spiritual dimension in as many different ways and as often as possible.

The Kabbalists felt that too much ritual was being taken for granted and not enough spirituality was being invested even in religious practices. They borrowed from the custom of 'inviting' to say grace by adding a meditation before every single religious act in order to encourage deeper consciousness and spirituality. The meditation before any act begins 'Behold, I am ready and prepared to carry out the will of God', and then the act is specified. The meditation goes on to assert that this is a way of uniting God with humanity and bringing the energies of a higher and more powerful realm into the human world.

## FOOD

The Bible, in Leviticus chapter 11 (repeated in Deuteronomy 14), gives laws about what animals, birds and fish may be eaten. Animals must have a split hoof and chew the cud, fish must have fins and scales, and in the case of birds no formula is given, but all birds of prey are excluded. What birds are allowed has become a matter of tradition. All kinds of ingenious explanations have been offered as to what lies behind these laws, hygiene, commercial or pagan taboo. No theory satisfies completely. For Jews these laws are statutes that need no logical reason but are a way of serving God and developing a degree of consciousness about one's actions, through eating, in the way one does through every other activity.

### Shechita (Ritual Slaughter)

The Bible bans drinking blood. Jacob's fight with the Angel that resulted in his being crippled is the basis given for the tradition of not eating the sinew that runs down the inside of the thigh. These, together with the forbidden animals, birds and fish, not eating pure fats or mixing meat products with milk, make up the dietary laws. The tradition of slaughtering animals in a particular way, although not specified in the Torah, is probably as old.

Since cruelty to animals is one of the universal laws the Talmud applies to the sons of Noah, it is understood that the aim of religious slaughter, *Shechita*, is to cause as little suffering as possible. It also aims to obviate serious damage to the major internal organs of an animal or bird in the process of slaughter. Its additional function is to remove as much arterial blood as possible from the animal.

The main artery that pumps blood to the brain is nearest to the surface at the neck. It runs alongside the supply of oxygen to the brain as well. An exceedingly sharp knife, the *chalaf,* which has to be inspected constantly for the slightest imperfection, is passed through the artery and windpipe and this effects an immediate drop of blood supply to the brain, causing instant blackout. The blood is drained away and this is the way the animal dies.

The objection to stunning, electrification and other methods is that they are not guaranteed to work every time and there is every likelihood that brain damage is caused in such a way that both causes pain and affects the internal organs. One thinks of the electric chair used for capital punishment in parts of America, which sometimes does not work as intended. An animal, even when killed in the correct manner, cannot be eaten if it is in anyway unhealthy or damaged. This is why Jews have difficulty with so-called 'humane' methods. On the other hand, although sharing certain common features, Hallal meat is not acceptable because the added refinements of shechita are absent.

It is the firm conviction of Jewish experts that shechita is the least painful of the methods available. When a human cuts his flesh the cutting itself, say with a razor blade, does not hurt. It is only when the sides of the cut are agitated that we feel pain. So this is assumed to be the case when a sharp blade severs the animal's artery. After the animal is killed its blood is drained and the forbidden fats removed. Then it must be washed and salted to remove remaining arterial blood before it can be cooked and eaten.

## Vegetarianism

There have been great rabbis in previous generations who were vegetarians for various reasons, most notably the first Chief Rabbi of Israel, Isaac Hacohen Kook. Many felt that the very idea of killing an animal outside the Temple was not ideal. Others disliked the process of leading animals to slaughter. Most rabbinic opinion tended to resist this on the grounds that the temple service was divinely ordained and God must have approved. The great Maimonides declared, in his *Guide to the Perplexed,* that animal sacrifices had been introduced at a time when they were the natural method of worship in order to wean people away from idolatry. Most Ultra-Orthodox rabbis have rejected the implications of this, that sacrifices were temporary as a reaction against modernism. As a result vegetarianism is most definitely a minority interest in Judaism, although, as everywhere, it is certainly becoming more common.

## Other Dietary Restrictions

It has been argued that the dietary laws were designed to keep Jews apart. But there is nothing intrinsic to the laws that should prevent a Jew sharing his or her food with anyone. Ironically, a much later series of rabbinic innovations was intended to achieve a measure of separation.

The Talmud records new laws designed to prevent intermarriage with pagans. These included not drinking wine, and not eating bread, olive oil or a banquet prepared by a pagan. Some of these restrictions fell into disuse right away simply on practical grounds. Others, particularly that concerning wine, have remained in force. These same laws and others were also given to prevent the learned classes from eating with the ignorant, even if they were Jewish. The overriding design was to strengthen the community of scholars and the law against those with no standards or morals.

The whole process of eating and preparing food was a creative activity that should add spirituality to what was otherwise a simple physical process. To underline this, the rabbis introduced laws requiring most eating and cooking vessels to be dedicated to a higher order by dipping them in the mikva, the ritual bath, which, as we will see, in many ways symbolised the transition from mundane to holy activity. Eating can be seen as a simple animal process of ingesting, absorbing and expelling. The function of these eating rituals is to try to elevate simple processes and make them opportunities to reflect on and be conscious of things we tend to take for granted.

There is a separate law that forbids eating or drinking anything that may be dangerous or unhealthy. So that even if food has passed all the hurdles mentioned above, one may still not be able to eat it if there is any danger at all. Modern scientific evidence of any harmful additive or process has a halachic basis for being taken very seriously. Similarly, evidence of harm from tobacco or any drug is halachic grounds for forbidding its use. To quote the Torah, 'And you shall take great care of yourselves.'

## STUDY

One cannot underestimate the importance of daily study in Judaism as a spiritual not just an intellectual process, an obligation that falls on everyone. The importance of education has been reiterated by the Torah itself and by succeeding generations of authorities. Morning prayers start with the blessing before study, and sections of the Talmud were introduced to ensure that at least a nominal amount of Torah was studied daily. The repetition of the Shema each day includes the statement, 'And you shall teach these words [the Torah] to your children and you should talk about them at home, on the way, morning and night time.' Throughout rabbinic literature, study is the most repeated obligation. But this is no academic exercise. The revealed word of God contains the clues, so it was felt, to understanding the Divine and therefore is as important an act of worship as prayer, if not more so.

Study is regarded as essential precisely because it is supposed to lead to good deeds. Any study that does not is considered empty (Mishna *Avot* 3.12, 22). Important as study is, there are other priorities. So if one is studying, and a wedding or a funeral passes by, one has an obligation to break off study. Similarly if the demands of a poor or suffering human are presented, then study and prayer are set aside.

The message is clear. A spiritual relationship with God is not compatible with neglecting His creatures. Spirituality and study are only means to an end, not an end in themselves. There was a time when it could have been said that the great Chassidic schism led to a divide between the Mitnagdim, who asserted the primary nature of study, and the Chassidim, who preferred prayer and ecstasy. This no longer applies as all sections have come to realise that study is the best guarantee of continuity, provided of course that one does not lose sight of the needs of humanity.

## RABBINIC AUTHORITY

There is no class of priests in Judaism or scholars who have a monopoly on learning or interpretation. The titular priesthood is kept alive only symbolically as a reminder of the past. Indeed there is nothing a rabbi can do that an ordinary layman cannot. The role of rabbi as practised in many communities today owes much to the Christian model of the priest as the servant of the community, or the provider of pastoral or ritual activities. Technically a rabbi is simply a teacher, and anyone can become a teacher. One does not need a rabbi in Judaism to conduct services or perform ritual ceremonies. Ideally each person should study enough not to need to consult a rabbi on matters of Jewish law, except in rare situations. Even where a rabbi is consulted, he cannot do other than refer to his sources in Jewish law in order to give a response. There is, for example, no Jewish equivalent of 'dispensation'. Each individual has to follow Jewish law; no one can relieve him or her of obligations. However, Jewish law is remarkably flexible in many respects and allows for exceptional situations. This is when a rabbinical expert comes in useful in finding ways within the law that others may be ignorant of.

In the talmudic past the term rabbi was applied to a scholar who had received instruction from someone handing down the oral tradition in a direct line from the Sanhedrin. This chain was lost and many great scholars refused to use this title. Indeed the greatest of all religious leaders were known by their first names. Later on, the title (in all local varieties and variations) was revived to meet the needs of secular authorities that wanted to appoint Jewish religious leaders to represent the religion. However, great rabbinic experts emerge today as they always have done on the basis of their learning and saintliness rather than by qualifying (except in Chassidic circles where leaders are usually dynastic).

Today there is a real distinction between rabbis functioning in communities and great rabbinic experts and scholars. It is almost as though there are two levels of rabbis, those who go out to teach or hold public positions and those more academic specialists who are almost unanimously held in high regard, but are often more removed from the average person. There is another category of qualification and this is the *Dayan* (Judge). In Israel religious judges are paid by the state and enjoy a higher status and salary than ordinary rabbis. In the Diaspora a Dayan is usually a rabbi who sits on a Beth Din, a Court of Law, and has additional expertise in certain areas such as marriage and divorce or civil damages.

Their followers revere Chassidic *rebbes* (heads of dynasties) to an amazing degree. They will be consulted on virtually every issue in a follower's life from whom to marry to where to invest. They will be asked about medical issues, as well as political and social policies. They may not themselves be rabbinical experts, but they will have a team of advisors and consultants to whom they may turn.

## BUSINESS AND OTHER ETHICS

The Torah repeats that honesty in business is one of the basic features of human behaviour that is essential for long life. 'You shall have honest weights and measures in order that you should live long on this earth' (Deuteronomy 25.13). The biblical concept of *Kiddush HaShem* (Sanctifying God's Name) implies that any behaviour that casts aspersions on Jews is to be avoided. Anything that brings Judaism or God into disrepute is one of the major misdemeanours that, according to the Talmud, even the Day of Atonement cannot atone for and affects one's afterlife as well. According to the Talmud, when a person dies he will be asked whether 'he carried out his business affairs with honesty'. Indeed, the volumes of the Talmud dealing with commerce, condemning dishonest business practices and establishing equitable trading conditions occupy a very significant part of the talmudic process and are amongst the most commonly studied folios in talmudic academies. The ability to participate in normal commercial practices outside Judaism simply reflects the internal obligations of Judaism towards others.

The biblical ban on lending for interest was precisely because lending money was considered part of the charitable process rather than the commercial As commercial practice changed, the rabbis of the Talmud began to modify biblical restrictions in a number of areas. Over time, ways were found to get round the interest laws by using a mechanism called the *Heter Isska* (permission to trade), which made the lender a sleeping partner in the borrower's business.

## CHARITY

Charity is also one of the most often repeated obligations of the Torah. Apart from the system of tithes, the requirement to help the poor is repeated more than any other law in the Torah. One is obliged to give at least a tenth of one's income to charity and there is a great deal of discussion as to whether one includes taxes gross or net and whether such charitable money may be used for education. No one, however poor, is exempt, but on the other hand there is a limit to how much one can give so as to avoid impoverishing oneself.

Those who are better off financially are expected to play a greater part in the charitable life of their community. The connection between charity and business exercises a strong influence on attitudes to wealth. Being able to accumulate wealth carries with it the obligation to help others. Making a poor man self-sufficient or enabling someone to set up a business to support himself and his family is the highest form of charity. Jewish communities are required by law to establish funds for the poor and *Gabbaey Tsedaka* (charity officers), who must always work in pairs to avoid suspicion, are regarded very highly within the community.

## JEWS AND NON-JEWS

The Bible did indeed draw a distinction between one's behaviour towards those people who shared the basic Torah values, one's neighbour or friend, and those who did not. It established the equivalent of citizenship rights. But it allowed for the stranger to live amongst the people on the assumption that he or she accepted certain basic principles and then had rights and could expect protection and justice. The pagan world was regarded as a world with no ethical values, without justice or a legal system.

The Talmud developed the principle of the son of Noah. He was a non-Jew who was not interested in converting but wanted to live within a Jewish community. This required adherence to the seven Noachide commandments. These principles differentiated between non-Jews and defined those one had to treat as civil equals and those one did not. It established the conditions for an 'an open legal system'. Common standards of justice were also the basis for fair and open economic activity.

According to the Talmud one must even treat pagans, let alone ethically committed non-Jews, with care and do nothing to alienate them. Hence, one allows them access to charity; one treats and cares for them so as to avoid ill feeling. Despite the years of oppression and ill- treatment of the Jews by both Christian and Muslim societies, there is not one rabbinic authority that did not consider theft from or misrepresentation to a non-Jew as being of equal odium as to a Jew. Sources that differentiate are intended purely academically to establish the nature of involvement with someone who shares spiritual values, as opposed to someone who does not. One might compare this to the rights that citizenship bestows on a member of one society as opposed to a visitor.

Judaism places great emphasis on ritual behaviour. However, this in no way detracts from the importance of ethical behaviour. One simply has to notice the constant repetition in the Bible of the importance of ethical be-haviour and the number of laws, notably in Leviticus, devoted to it. It is, however, left to God to judge the inner secrets of mankind.

## SIN AND ATONEMENT

Throughout Jewish religious literature there are many different attempts to explain the origin of sin and evil. There is no dogma in Judaism of the 'fall of man' or a 'state of sin'. The biblical words for sin are *Cheyt*, derived from the word meaning to 'miss the mark', *Aveyra* from 'turning off the path', *Avon* to 'be missing something', and *Pesha* 'to falter'. All these words imply that if something has gone wrong, one simply needs to put it right in order to return to a state of equilibrium.

In Temple times sacrifices played the primary role in dealing with faults. First one had to confess (before God, but not man) and specify the action and regret. Then one could bring an offering as atonement. This assumed that in matters relating to other human beings restitution or compensation was paid because without this any attempt at atonement was useless. The biblical command that a thief pays double (four and five times the value of livestock) only applied if the thief did not repent and was caught in possession. The Day of Atonement seems originally to have been more of a national day of atonement than one for individuals.

There is a debate amongst the medieval rabbis as to whether repentance, *Teshuva*, had a separate function. Maimonides summed up the debate and concluded that since the destruction of the Temple, Teshuva had become the main vehicle for individuals to restore the balance with God. However, there are some misdemeanours that require the Day of Atonement to complete the process, and yet others where only death seals the atonement (desecrating God's name is one example and this underlines the importance of daily ethical behaviour).

The result of all this is that Judaism places tremendous emphasis on a person's responsibility. There is little weight given in Judaism to the idea of people having intermediary roles in the relationship with God. There has always been a tradition of some people being on a higher spiritual level than others, going back to the time of Abraham. Their role has always been to guide individuals towards greater self-fulfilment, not act on their behalf (although some tendencies in the Chassidic world tend to indicate otherwise).

## CHOSEN PEOPLE

A great deal has been made, usually by people outside Judaism, of the idea of 'the Chosen People', even though it plays no theological role in Jewish thinking. Understood in the context of the biblical narrative, it simply means that if the nation follows the ethical and spiritual demands of God they will then have a relationship with Him. No major Jewish thinker has ever suggested that it implies automatic superiority, indeed superiority of any kind. If anything, the idea implies an obligation to live a good life and to set a good example. In the way that 'witness' in Christianity confers no notion of automatic superiority so, in Judaism, the idea of a special relationship with God confers nothing automatically. The very fact that Jews have been exiled and suffered for their failures shows clearly that the relationship is reciprocal rather than automatic. Ideas such as these serve to make a Jew aware, daily, of his and her obligation to live a full and spiritual life in accordance with the guidelines laid down in the Torah and its extensions. The covenant made on Sinai remains the covenant that Jews are bound by and is the moving spirit behind daily practice.

## LIVING UNDER OTHER SYSTEMS

Exile created new realities for the Jewish people. The Talmud accepts the fact that Jews will live under alien regimes. As a result it established the principle that 'the Law of the Land is the Law'. This was applied specifically to commercial and then civil matters. Nevertheless, a Jew is required to resort to Jewish courts of law for civil claims before going to the state courts. In theory religious issues had to reign supreme and if there were to be a clash, then one would have to find another home.

The issue came to a head during the Spanish Inquisition. Many Jews fled, but others converted. These *conversos* (the derogatory Spanish term was *marrano*, pig) were not regarded as having betrayed their religion and when they arrived in freer communities they were welcomed back into the fold automatically. The Spanish experience led to a tendency amongst Jews to try to fit into parent societies as much as possible. In matters of dress and convention they tended to adopt the patterns and customs of their host societies very quickly. This was best illustrated by the German Jewish maxim, 'A Jew at home, a German in the street'.

This was the general tendency until the Second World War. Subsequently, societies have changed and in the West have become much more multicultural. As a result, more and more Jews feel able to mix openly in society while still retaining their specific modes of dress and behaviour. The Jewish world today is divided between those Jews who try not to distinguish themselves from their host societies and those who feel comfortable enough, or ideologically committed enough, to appear different.

The Jewish day begins and ends by combining an awareness of one's physicality with the presence of a spiritual dimension. This why before going to sleep one recites the Shema. The last thoughts of the day should be of God.

# Chapter 6

# The Jewish Life Cycle

Every important stage in a person's life is marked with a ceremony. Just as the function of Judaism in daily life is to try to make as many mundane actions as possible special and occasions for reflection, so too the passages in life are marked out to be recognised and valued.

## BIRTH

There is a debate in the Talmud as to when the soul enters a child. The Roman position was that it entered the body at conception, the Jewish at birth. This is one of the few issues where, over time, Jewish attitudes have tended towards the Roman position. However, in legal terms a child is only recognised as an independent being after the head and the majority of its body has emerged from the womb. Until then, it is regarded as a limb of its mother whose existing life takes precedence. This does not mean that the foetus has no status at all. It can only be interfered with if the mother's life is in danger (some modern authorities would include psychological damage or a threat to the mother's health).

Eight days after birth, a male child is circumcised. This is based on Genesis chapter 17 verse 10. The ceremony is called the *Brit* (literally 'The Covenant'). It is performed by a *mohel,* a circumciser. Anyone can train for this honoured role and follows a rigorous training and apprenticeship. If there is any possibility of physical danger the circumcision is delayed, but otherwise it takes place whatever the occasion, even on Shabbat or Yom Kippur.

The Friday night beforehand is nowadays, following the kabbalistic tradition, called the *Shalom Zachar* (the welcoming of the male) and a celebration is held in the parents' home after the Friday evening meal. The custom is not mentioned until post-medieval texts. It is a means of enabling the community to participate in celebrating the birth, particularly for those who may not be free to attend the Brit itself.

The brit ceremony is performed as early on the eighth day as possible (often after the morning service while the father is still wrapped in his tefillin and talit) and is followed by a *seudat mitzvah,* a celebratory meal at which, as always, wine is drunk and special blessings celebrate the occasion. Circumcision remains a powerful symbol of Jewish identity. Medical arguments in favour (or against) circumcision in general are irrelevant religiously. The rite is as old as Judaism and a link with the past. It is the supreme physical act of faith and commitment, the symbolic extension of Abraham's willingness to sacrifice his son to God. The blood of the covenant replaced child sacrifice and is the symbol of human creativity that parallels the female blood of the womb.

## BAR MITZVAH

According to biblical law a person is not considered a responsible or punishable citizen until he is thirteen if male, or twelve and a half if female. This applies both to civil and to ritual responsibility. Until this moment the child is regarded as the responsibility of the parent, in all civil and ritual matters. There is no special ceremony attached to this coming of age recorded in the texts until well after the Talmud; then the expression is that a child has reached the stage of having to keep the *mitzvot*, the commandments. To mark this transition, a child was called to read from the Torah and so give expression to his new role in the community by doing something he could not hitherto.

Over the years a more sophisticated ceremony emerged in which a child showed his developing intellectual prowess by giving a lecture on a talmudic theme. An alternative was to have the child read from the Torah itself. The event would be followed by a celebratory meal.

In many sectors of the Jewish world the Bar Mitzvah has become an occasion for celebration with little religious significance. The scholarly lecture has been replaced by a general 'thank you' speech, the *seudat mitzva* meal by a party and dance, which more often than not marks the end of a child's religious involvement rather than the beginning. The female version, the *Bat Mitzvah*, is a recent development that owes more to the need to encourage female involvement in modern religious life than to tradition. It is used as a way of encouraging girls to continue their Jewish studies. It is disregarded altogether by the very Orthodox.

## MARRIAGE

The biblical tradition does not record any kind of ritual to do with a wedding ceremony. Intercourse was considered the basis of conjugality. But the Torah distinguishes between the stage of *erusin*, binding commitment, and *nissuin*, actual marriage. Marriage was a transaction (albeit with obligations to the wife, which had to be honoured and were supported by law) and a father had rights over his under-age daughter. The Bible allows for divorce (Deuteronomy 24) and includes the obligation of the Levirate marriage, wherein a dead brother's childless wife is married to the next brother so that the name of the dead brother is kept alive.

Talmudic law was incredibly innovative in two areas. It insisted there should be a ceremony of marriage, the *Chuppa*. In addition, it introduced a contract, the *ketuba*, which guaranteed financial support to the wife in the event of death or divorce and protected her own assets. Although monogamy was the preferred state of the talmudic rabbis, it was not until the first millennium that Rabbeynu Gershon, the accepted European authority in the tenth century, accepted the practice. Although the Sepharadi world did not accept his authority, monogamy now applies throughout the Jewish world.

The Chuppa ceremony combines the erusin and nissuin stages into one ceremony. As with all religious ceremonies, it is performed over wine and there are two cups that distinguish the two sections. After the couple drink from the first cup of wine, the bridegroom puts a ring on his bride's finger. This seals the agreement and the ketuba is then read out aloud to the gathering.

The rabbis introduced seven blessings, the *sheva brachot*, that add a poetic and spiritual dimension. These are sung or said over the second cup of wine. Finally, a glass is broken to record the sadness of life as well as its joy and the destruction of the Temple. These are the essentials of the traditional ceremony. Each community adds its own embellishments. In some eastern communities there are very elaborate bridal ceremonies that can go on for days before the wedding. In western communities these are confined to the bridal reception and the 'bedecking of the bride' before the ceremony. The bedecking involves the bridegroom bringing down the veil to cover his bride. Originally this was what the Chuppa meant. Later on, it was the ceremony where the bride gave her assent to the marriage. In some communities this was the only opportunity for the couple see each other before they got married. This is the basis of the myth that the bedecking is to ensure that the bride is the right one, since in Jacob's first marriage he thought he was marrying Rachel, but in fact got Leah.

Different communities have different musical traditions and different ways of leading the bride under the Chuppa. In traditional communities the bride dedicates her husband by walking around him seven times in the way that many dedications of holiness, one thinks of the Temple in particular, involve a procession that goes around the object or territory that is being sanctified seven times. Often the rabbi gives a sermon and then the traditional ceremony continues. After it is all over the couple retire to a *cheder yichud* (the room of intimacy) where they are left alone for a while before facing the reception and banquet.

The Talmud emphasises the importance of celebrating the meal as part of a specific command that applies to everyone to 'make the bride and bridegroom happy'. Rabbis and teachers dance and sing the praises of the couple. The seven blessings are then repeated. This goes on each evening at parties that continue for six more days (though in more assimilated communities these additional parties are often abandoned in favour of a 'honeymoon', often far away from anyone who might want to join in the celebrations).

On the day of the ceremony, the couple fast until the ceremony itself. The marriage ceremony initiates a new era in the couple's life and, like the Day of Atonement, acts to erase the past. The wedding 'creates' a new couple in many senses, including the spiritual.

## THE MIKVAH

The bride (and sometimes the bridegroom) will have gone to the mikva before the Chuppa. The mikva is a very important element in Jewish sexual life. It is a pool of natural water. Natural pools, rivers or seas may also be considered as mikvas provided they contain sufficient natural water. The Bible stresses the importance for anyone wanting to enter the sanctuary of being 'clean' in a ritual sense. This is not a matter of hygiene because one has to be completely clean before beginning the ceremony of immersion. It has more to do with a spiritual preparation and renewal. As Noah's flood washed away one state of the world and initiated another, so the mikva symbolises changes in spiritual status rather than in physical status. An unmarried woman is called a *nida*. The Bible bans intercourse with a nida and only the mikva marks the transition from a forbidden to an allowed condition. After marriage a woman becomes a nida again with her monthly period. The rabbis added a five-day statutory interval that defined the nida and the seven clear days waiting interval before a woman could go to the mikva.

Sometimes the period may go on for longer. During this time not only sex but physical contact is also forbidden. All sorts of medical and sexual reasons are offered to justify this tradition, both in physical terms of protecting against certain infections and of enhancing the magic of a relationship through enforced separation. But the committed Jew obeys these laws out of obedience to the Torah rather than for any benefits that might accrue.

Sex is regarded as a divine gift and a pleasure to be enjoyed. According to the Bible, if a man does not provide for his wife's sexual pleasure he will have failed in his obligations and this could even be the basis for annulling the marriage. The Talmud rules that between husband and wife anything is allowed sexually so long as there is agreement and no coercion. This is the accepted legal position. There is indeed a long and strong tradition of modesty in Judaism and particularly during sex. There is no truth at all to the myth that the very Orthodox make love through a hole in a sheet.

There is a biblical obligation to reproduce. According to the school of Shammai, one should have two boys, but according to Hillel having a boy and a girl meet the obligation. In general the Talmud disapproves of contraception, except in cases of a danger to health, but after having had the requisite number of children the rabbinic attitude towards contraception is less negative. Conditions such as famine, according to the Talmud, require one to desist from reproduction, but otherwise one is encouraged to continue. A childless couple is allowed to divorce and try with other partners, but they are not forced to divorce against their wishes.

## DIVORCE

The Bible recognises divorce. The Talmud even encourages it where there is tension and ill feeling (assuming all obligations to women and children are met). Nevertheless, divorce issues represent a major problem in Jewish life because both parties are required to agree and where one refuses this can lead to complications.

A bill of divorce, the *Get*, has to be ordered by the husband to be written for his wife and then it must be handed to her. The initial marriage document, the Ketuba, was designed to ensure that in the case of divorce a woman would not be left without provision so that she would not lose status or be forced to rely on the charity of her family. But there were cases, such as adultery, where a woman could lose her Ketuba rights. The husband is required to go before a Beth Din, a court of law, and delegate the court scribe to write the Get, after which the court will convey it to the woman. The Beth Din then calls in the woman and 'hands' the Get to her. In countries where there is a civil system regulating these matters, the Beth Din does not hand over the Get until the civil divorce has been finalised.

Another type of divorce relates to the Levirate marriage, *Yibum*, which requires a man to marry the wife of a childless dead brother. In biblical times it protected the woman and gave her options. For the past thousand years the right to marry one's sister-in-law has been abandoned. However, in such situations the ceremony called *Chalitza* (relinquishing responsibility) has to be performed by the brother. This too is a form of divorce and if he refuses the widow cannot remarry.

Problems arise when a man refuses to give a divorce, a Get or Chalitza, or when he disappears with no trace. In such situations the wife becomes an *Agunah*, an abandoned wife. This is one of the sources of tension within traditional Judaism between the ecclesiastical authorities and the increasing number of campaigners on behalf of women's rights within Judaism. Another is the tendency of the Beth Din, the religious court, to favour the male in matters of custody over the children and property rights. Comparing custody judgements passed by secular and religious courts in Israel has highlighted this bias.

Originally, Jewish ecclesiastical authorities forced reluctant husbands to agree to give a divorce. But as their powers disappeared during the dispersion they no longer had this ability. Although it is true that a woman needs to agree too, the rabbis have found ways for men to get round this, whereas similar attempts to help women have been rejected. Currently, secular law courts are relied upon to ensure that civil divorce is not granted until religious divorces are granted.

If a woman remarries without a religious divorce she is still considered married to the first husband by Jewish law. Any new children will then be regarded as *mamzerim*. This is not the same as a 'bastard', an illegitimate child in secular law, because in Judaism this status only applies to the children of a marriage forbidden by the Torah, not say to someone born out of wedlock.

Most Reform Jews no longer require the Get or Chalitza. This has created a serious rift in Jewish life because it means that in religious terms there has been no divorce and the first couple are still married. This then has ramifications for the children who become mamzerim. Traditional Jews would not allow marriage to the children of remarried divorcees.

The Reform community has accepted patrilineal descent, defining Judaism through the father in addition to the mother. Traditional Jews who adhere to a matrilineal definition do not accept this criterion. Reform apologists argue that the matrilineal definition of Judaism is a late one, historically. Tribal affiliation in the Bible was and is through the father. On the other hand, traditionalists argue that the definition of a Jew through the mother nationally, as opposed to tribally, is of biblical origin.

Together these two issues have, for the first time since the Samaritans, created a fundamental split within Jewry, almost akin to the Catholic-Protestant schism in Christianity.

## DEATH

Visiting the sick is regarded in the Talmud as one of the most important of Jewish laws. Most communities have groups of volunteers whose job it is to visit hospitals or those who are ill and help in any way possible. All measures may be used to relieve pain, but nothing may be done, according to Jewish law, to hasten death. Euthanasia or suicide are forbidden. Once a person has died the body is treated with great respect since it was host to the soul, often described as 'a part of God above'. For this reason, all human body parts have to be buried and cremation is unacceptable to traditional Jews.

The dead body is watched over until it is handed to the *Chevra Kaddisha*, the 'holy society', probably the most honoured volunteer group of Jewish men and women. The body is washed, dressed in white shrouds, and placed in a coffin in the Diaspora, but straight into the earth in Israel. The burial takes place as soon as possible and only civil state requirements, such as a criminal autopsy, are allowed to delay burial.

Jews are allowed to donate organs to save life or for other immediate emergencies. In practice there is some reluctance to become general donors for fear that body parts may be used for experiments or treated casually. But where one's organs may save a life, it is universally accepted that this is the right thing to do.

On hearing bad news there is a blessing 'recognising God as just judge'. When a close relative or great rabbi dies the custom is to make a symbolic tear in one's clothes, called *Keriah*. For parents and children the tear is on the right side, for others it is on the left. Mourners are comforted initially at the grave, but after the funeral they gather at home for a seven-day period called the *Shiva* (literally 'seven') during which they sit on low stools as visitors keep them company and prepare their food for them. Only Shabbat or a festival allow for a break.

Starting at the burial mourners recite *Kaddish*. They continue saying Kaddish at services for eleven months in the case of parents, one month for other close relatives. The Kaddish is not a special mourners' prayer. Its meaning, 'sanctification', is a very general word that also applies to the ceremony of welcoming in a festival. Kaddish is also used to mark stages in the course of a service. Nothing in it refers to death. It is simply a poetic tribute to the greatness of God. Originally mourners were encouraged to study in order to 'compensate' the community for the loss of one of its members. Then they were expected to conduct services. As that too became more difficult, they were allocated the simplest and most familiar part of the service that had the added advantage of being in Aramaic, which was the vernacular for most Jews 2,000 years ago.

Mourning lasts for a year for parents. During this time they recite Kaddish, do not shave or cut hair (relaxed after thirty days), do not participate in any joyous occasion where music is played, do not buy new articles – and, strictly speaking, they should not exchange greetings. For other relatives the mourning period lasts for thirty days.

The anniversary of a death is called the *YaarZeit* in Yiddish (anniversary). Traditionally, this was kept as a fast, but kabbalistic and chassidic traditions have felt it was more appropriate to celebrate the soul's journey to a 'happier' world and arrange a small reception in the synagogues or shtiebel in honour of the departed.

It is natural, on the one hand, to fear death. The Psalmist points out that 'the dead cannot praise God.' The basic human response is indeed to recoil. However much Judaism emphasises the importance of living and the value of life, the fact is that death is regarded in many ways as a release to a higher level. The fear of judgement, for better or for worse, is used a great deal in liturgy. Ideas regarding death vary greatly in the Jewish tradition, but the tendency is to think positively in terms of passing over into 'the world of truth' and to welcome the process while regretting leaving one's loved ones behind.

## CONVERSION

It is clear from biblical narratives that Judaism welcomed people who wanted to join. The Bible mentions the stranger, the Ger, a great deal in many different contexts. Rabbinic terminology differentiated two types of Ger. The *Ger Toshav* (the stranger living amongst you) was given equal civil rights, but it is uncertain whether there was any kind of ceremony. The *Ger Tsedek* (the righteous stranger) is a later concept that now is applied specifically to a convert.

The Book of Ruth illustrates the perfect example of an ideological convert. The Judean kings married for political reasons. It was Ezra who first issued an ultimatum to the priests to 'put away their strange wives'.

Throughout the mishnaic period conversion was welcomed and great rabbis such as Shemaya and Avtalyon, teachers of Hillel, were converts. One of the greatest Aramaic scholars of the Bible was Aquila the Convert. Some rabbis were opposed to going out to proselytise, but the Talmud contains far more quotes in favour of converts than against them. There is a series of stories concerning the differences in attitude to conversion between Hillel and Shammai. A pagan asking to convert if he can be taught the Written Law, but not the Oral Law, or in another case if he can be taught the Torah standing on one leg, is rejected by Shammai but welcomed by Hillel.

Judaism made significant inroads into Roman society 2,000 years ago. Many Romans who rejected paganism found Judaism an attractive alternative. Early Christian proselytisers often went to synagogues where potential converts gathered. A monotheistic alternative with fewer ritual limitations was an attraction that early Christianity succeeded in tapping into.

However, there were two other very important factors that affected the Jewish attitude to conversion. Judah Maccabee and his bothers had carried out a series of raids initially to defend beleaguered Jewish communities but then had forcibly converted several tribes to Judaism. Forced converts entered the community; they were known as 'converts by lions' because they only converted out of fear. Nevertheless, they played an important role in Jewish society. The man responsible for terminating the Hasmonean dynasty, Herod, was himself descended from Idumean forced converts. Given the poor relations between the Hasmoneans and the rabbis, their jaundiced view of forced conversions had a basis.

There was not the same impetus to convert from an ideological point of view as in Christianity or Islam. Judaism did and indeed does not believe that only Jews are saved and everyone else ends up in purgatory or in eternal damnation. The Talmud establishes two important principles. One is that 'the pious of the nations have a place in the world to come.' This means that one does not have to be Jewish to be 'saved'. So long as one keeps the seven basic commandments that the Talmud says were given to the sons of Noah, one could achieve similar spiritual levels.

Maimonides does draw a distinction between the 'wise of the nations' and the 'pious of the nations'. The former arrive at truth through intellect; they are to be praised, but not as much as those who accept divine authority as a matter of faith. Jewish proselytisers were animated not because they thought that they were going to save the world or its citizens from damnation, but simply because they felt that their way to God was an advantageous and effective one.

After Constantine the world slowly became hostile to Judaism and in most of the Christian world it became an offence to convert to Judaism, punishable by death. The same thing happened under Islam. As a result Judaism started turning in on itself and conversion became rare. A would-be convert is asked, 'Why do you want to join the Jewish people? Do you not know we a small and downtrodden and life is hard for us?' But if he or she persists, a convert has to be welcomed. There are many examples of Christians converting to Judaism. But a good many of them, from places as far apart as medieval Oxford and eighteenth-century Portugal, were burnt at the stake for their pains.

The Enlightenment and assimilation created new problems. Intermarriage meant that many Jews who married non-Jewish spouses wanted to convert to please others or to gain social membership of the Jewish people. Traditional rabbis only accepted conversion out of conviction. For many of them, a conversion out of convenience was a mockery. For others, it was seen as an opportunity to bring someone into the Jewish fold. This remains the case today. The Jewish world is divided between those groups who make life easy for converts and welcome non-Jewish spouses, and those who will only accept a convert out of commitment to an intense Jewish lifestyle.

Israel's desire to encourage immigration has led to a more conciliatory approach that argues that as Judaism is the dominant religion it exercises a subtle influence. One can be easier on those who choose to live in Israel. The difficulty is that often such converts have found they face problems in some Diaspora communities if they do not practise traditional Judaism.

Once a convert is accepted, males are circumcised and both men and women go to the mikva where immersion in water symbolises a new era. From that moment onwards, it is a contravention of Jewish law to mistreat or discriminate against a convert, or even to mention a convert's past.

## WOMEN

In the modern world all religions come under scrutiny for the way they treat women. There are two biblical narratives in Genesis chapters 1 and 2. The first has man and woman created simultaneously. The second describes woman as coming from man's rib. The first chapter describes the 'ingredients of the world', the second deals with interactions. So in terms of creation, male and female lives are equal. However in terms of the way society works, in biblical times men took the primary role. The Torah describes a 'man's world' with the male taking the leadership roles, deciding the tribal possessions, and commanding the judicial systems.

In biblical legislation no distinction was made between the sexes on issues of ritual or worship. In those Temple functions open to the laity, there was no difference in obligation or access between the sexes. The only distinctions were between priest and layperson, and Israel and the pagan world. Similarly, no distinction was made between male and female in terms of civil damages or value of life. However, distinctions existed over matters of inheritance and marriage. Other variations existed as between males under twenty and over sixty and between women but this was restricted to one limited area. Although the case of the daughters of Zelophchad (Numbers 27) allowed female inheritance under some conditions thousands of years before it was possible in many western societies, nevertheless there were disadvantages.

The biggest issue was the unacceptability of women as witnesses in courts of law. The intent may well have been to protect female modesty and to limit exposure to the public eye. However, over time this became a means of putting women at a disadvantage. Despite this the Bible records female judges and prophets. In areas not subject to male appointment, charismatic women could excel. Similarly, wealthy women were also able to protect their interests.

The rabbis of the Talmud went to great lengths to ameliorate female disadvantages. The Ketuba, the marriage contract, was chief among them because it guaranteed certain basic rights and a financial settlement. It ensured that women had a claim on the estate even if it did pass to males. There were civil and legal innovations as well and the fact that women were playing a full role in commerce at the time is also reflected in protective talmudic commercial law. Nevertheless, women as a class were considered un-educated, just as the *Am HaAretz* (the ordinary peasant or ignoramus) was considered to be of lesser standing by the community of scholars. The fact that women were not given sufficient opportunities to study put them at a disadvantage. The Jewish world community defined itself socially either in terms of wealth or in terms of scholarship. This meant in practice that either of these avenues was available to both sexes as a means of rising or, equally, of being suppressed.

The rabbis introduced the principle that women were free from all laws related to obligations in time. The intention was that priority should be given to children and the home. During the Temple times this was not a problem because everyone had access to the Temple whenever they had the opportu-nity. But afterwards, the exclusion of women from the synagogue services would in time lead to a measure of ill feeling, particularly on the part of liberated women. From a male point of view, giving women responsibility for house and hearth was, in theory, simply strengthening the values and importance of family and home. The problems with this position did not arise when the husband treated his wife as an equal, but when he did not. The judicial system seemed to favour the husband, if not by law then certainly by sentiment. This is particularly relevant in matters of divorce and custody. The fact that every other society did the same at the time is cold comfort.

It is true that slowly, even in the most Orthodox of societies, the position of women is improving and the vast majority seem to be content with their lot. Pressure from secular society is beginning to have an effect. Yet it also causes retrenchment. Reform Judaism has removed any distinction between the sexes and as a result women are coming to play a dominant role both academically and ritually in Reform communities. Whilst in Orthodoxy more opportunities exist for women than hitherto, there is strong resistance to giving in to pressure that would allow secular and non-religious values to dictate the agenda.

Women increasingly contribute in social and academic areas, but not in rabbinic roles. Any society that feels itself under assault withdraws and becomes more defensive. Orthodoxy argues that women should concentrate on the home, yet they are allowed to work and have professions. Religious life should have its own values and not imitate others.

The crucial issue is how to bring about change. Orthodoxy will not allow change to Halacha and therefore there is no chance that it will alter the religious services. However, increasingly Orthodox women who want more participation are setting up their own spiritual alternatives, just as more and more Orthodox women are studying rabbinic texts and developing rabbinic expertise.

Meanwhile the importance of daily religious ritual in the home underlines the fact that, religiously speaking, the home is indeed more important than the synagogue. Only in less religiously committed communities does the synagogue become the central point of religious life.

## RESPONSIBILITY FOR PARENTS

Respect for parents is one of the Ten Commandments and a central issue in Jewish life. Parents have certain stated responsibilities for their children, but over a person's lifetime, these fall by the wayside. A parent has an obligation to marry off children or train them to earn a living, all specified in the Talmud. But a child's obligation to his parents is an ongoing one that interestingly falls primarily on the male in talmudic law. This is because of the assumption that the woman has neither the means nor the freedom to care for her parents. Of course, in a modern society, where both partners work, a different complexion is placed on the issue.

Responsibility is defined as having a financial as well as a moral obligation. The local Beth Din has the right to compel a man to support his parents. In Orthodox communities the synagogue or the study centres offer the opportunity for the elderly to remain part of the community in a productive way throughout their lives. The strong family culture also gives responsibility and authority to elder women. Unlike secular societies where a person's value is often determined by earning power or work, in Orthodox societies one is valued for a range of other qualities that enable one to contribute both to the family and the wider community, academically and socially, regardless of one's financial position. The strongly 'tribal' communities integrate the elderly effectively. They are valued as the transmitters of tradition to the younger generation. They become teachers and guides and are treated with respect and reverence; above all, they are made to feel needed and wanted.

The problems arise outside these strongly committed communities, or when families cannot or will not help. Here the strong communal ethic ensures that most Jewish communities provide homes and services for their elderly members. Throughout the Jewish world provision is made to look after those without families and to ensure that in old age it will be possible for them to live within communities that share similar values and customs.

# Chapter 7

# Jewish Theology

## IN THE TORAH

The Torah was written in a pre-theological era. Its preoccupation is with how a people behaves. This should not be taken to indicate that thought is unimportant, but rather that it is difficult to legislate for.

The first three of the Ten Commandments (Exodus 20) are often regarded as a distillation of biblical ideology, and they do help to introduce ideas about the relationship between man and God. The first of the commandments asserts that YHVH is the God who took the Children of Israel out of Egypt and only He may be worshipped. There is no attempt here to define or explain the nature of God or of belief. It is more a matter of fact or experience.

The second principle is that no other gods may be worshipped or images made. However, there is nothing here that helps with the definition of God. It continues with the idea that God responds to good and bad behaviour, but what does it mean when it says that God is 'a zealous God'? The Hebrew itself would better be translated as 'consequent' or 'consistent', rather than the more emotional and very human term 'zealous'. It means that bad or corrupt behaviour inevitably impacts on society and on the children who are affected by it. Similarly, good and ethical behaviour has a positive impact. This is not intended as a legislative principle because later on (Deuteronomy 24.16) the Torah emphasises that people are punished only for their own actions and not for those of others. This idea of 'consequence' is repeated over and over again throughout the Torah.

The third commandment is that God's name should not be taken in vain. This combines ideas of respect for God with the nature of oaths and vows. In earlier times one's word really needed to be one's bond. The court system was based on the assumption that one would not give false testimony and that if one took a vow this was as good as fact, a morally binding commitment. In such a situation, taking words as meaningless tools would have been unacceptable.

Using a person's name was not something to be taken lightly at a time when the Bible placed so much emphasis on name changes. So if this was the case with regard to humans, how much more so should it apply to God. Yet, the emphasis here is on human responses rather than divine ones.

Other biblical texts try to go further with phrases such as 'God is One' and 'No human can see God and live' (Exodus 33.20). God tells Moses in

Exodus, I AM WHAT I AM. Even if we take the Hebrew YHVH to mean something much more significant theologically, such as beyond time or not subject to change, or even 'I guarantee to keep my word', we may well wonder whether we are not imposing much later thought patterns on a different form of expression. What exactly did these phrases mean to those who heard them? In general, the divine relationship is portrayed in biblical language in very human, descriptive terms.

The Oral Law introduced other ideas not mentioned explicitly in the Torah, such as the afterlife, Messianism, and the eternity of the soul. Later rabbinic interpretation tried to establish that they were explicit as well as implicit. But even then, these ideas are introduced in Judaism in an unstructured form.

## IN THE MIDRASH

The way ideas are expressed in post-biblical Judaism is through Midrash. This is a system of exegesis and popular homiletics that either starts with a biblical text and expounds it, or with a law and then relates it to a religious message. The midrashic method is very different to the philosophical. Judaism quite consciously tried, in contrast to the Graeco-Roman way of thinking, to assert its own style.

The result is that there is no formulation of a systematic theological position. There are specific declarations, such as the mishnaic source in the *Sanhedrin* that 'All Israel has a place in the World To Come except for those who reject the idea that Resurrection is derived from the Torah', that the Torah comes from heaven and various other exclusions. The chapter goes on to deal with other issues such as Messianism. Elsewhere the Mishna discusses reward and punishment and the afterlife. But each time the ideas are mentioned in a cursive rather than an exhaustive way.

Throughout the talmudic period the debates that mattered to Jews were over authority. Was rabbinic authority usurped from the priests? Was rabbinic authority a new development or a continuation of the original revelation? What was the nature of the relationship between God and Israel? These were the issues that separated Judaism from the Samaritans and indeed the pagan world.

The apocalyptic traditions of the Dead Sea sects and the emergence of the Christian challenge called on Jewish thinkers to start defining the differences. Slowly a Jewish theology began to emerge. Philo of Alexandria wrote the first attempt to reconcile Judaism with Graeco-Roman society. It took another 900 years before Saadyah Gaon's *Emunot VeDeot*, written in Babylon, borrowed neo-Platonic arguments to explain Judaism. And then a real flowering of theological debate emerged under Islamic influence.

## POST-TALMUDIC THOUGHT

The greatest of the medieval Jewish philosophers Maimonides, born in Cordova in 1135 and then exiled to Egypt, has exercised the strongest influence on mainstream Jewish theology. His *Guide to the Perplexed*, written originally in Arabic and based on his Aristotelian way of thinking (though not following Aristotle on creation), remains unsurpassed in the realms of Jewish theological discourse. However, in his lifetime it was burnt and he was accused of heresy for simply studying philosophy and trying to reconcile the Torah with a non-Jewish system.

Maimonides had been called upon by Jews living in Christian and Muslim societies to help them defend themselves against the theological onslaughts of the established religions. He was not alone. In Spain Yehuda Halevy had written his *Kuzari* as an argument in favour of Judaism over its 'usurping children' Christianity and Islam. Nachmanides would soon after have to defend Judaism against Christian attacks supported by Isabella and Ferdinand.

Whereas Halevy and Nachmanides took a more mystical line, Maimonides based his arguments on solidly rational foundations. Yet even he, in the end, found himself giving priority to tradition over logic. His *Thirteen Principles of Faith*, accepted to this day by the Orthodox world, though not a required expression of faith in any ritual sense, are a convenient menu of the main theological issues in Judaism.

## GOD

Five of the thirteen principles are to do specifically with God. The idea of God as creator is explicit in the Torah. Unlike Aristotle, Maimonides sets out to prove that the world was created *ex nihilo*, out of nothing. His arguments, the ontological and the teleological, will be familiar to Christian theologians. Nevertheless, his innovation lies in the need to understand the biblical texts in other than superficial and simplistic ways. This laid the foundations for later attempts to reconcile scientific and evolutionary ideas with the narratives of the Torah. Just as, he argued, the expressions 'the Hand of God' or 'the Voice of God' did not necessarily mean that God had hands or vocal chords so too other anthropomorphisms in the Bible could not be taken literally.

The other issues he fought for in terms of describing God were those of unity and corporeality. The idea of God being 'One' was to Maimonides not a negative, there are not many Gods, only one, but a positive statement about the only perfect unity that is God. Yet he was anxious to assert that one cannot as a finite human say anything positive about the nature of God. One can only say what God is not. He also argued that God must be 'the First and the Last'. This issue was of importance to him within the context of contemporary philosophy. God had to be the Prime Mover and above and beyond all material considerations. This led to another principle that God could be the only object of worship.

Maimonides regarded the Islamic concept of Allah as being identical to the Jewish, but argued that the Christian Trinity was a betrayal of the divine unity. On this basis, he argued that Christianity retained the status of idolatry.

The flexibility of Jewish theology is illustrated by the response of the Menachem Ben Solomon, known as the Meiri of Provence (1249–1316), who argued that idolatry was not characterised by the nature of theological belief but by whether or not there was a moral and ethical code of behaviour.

Interestingly, Kabbalah had already developed the concept of the ten *Sephirot*, the ten emanations, as a way of explaining how a non-physical infinite force, *Ein Sof*, could interact with physical beings. If *Shechina*, the Divine Presence, is the vehicle of divine intervention in human affairs, how does the infinite transform itself in such a way as to relate to humans? The Sephirot were seen as aspects of a complex process of distillation that sought to explain why humans experience God in different ways. Opponents of Kabbalah argued that this was compounding the problem of the Christian Trinity, which at least reduced the Godhead to three. The Kabbalists replied that they were not describing the Godhead at all, but its manifestation.

Another of Maimonides' important principles was that God could have no physical form or representation. In Judaism, as well as in Islam, all images and forms were excluded from places of worship (even though in very early synagogues now excavated from the period around the first millennium there were mosaic images).

In biblical literary style, particularly in Isaiah and Ezekiel, the terms 'son of man' and in the Psalms, 'son of god' were simply ways of bestowing dignity on human beings, particularly prophetic ones. There is no tradition in Judaism at all of elevating human beings to superhuman status. Indeed it is very hard for Jews to understand the idea of God having a son in the way Christianity came to understand it. However, the issue that most preoccupied the Jewish philosophers was how to express the relationship with the Divine in spiritual and behavioural terms.

Nowadays within the Orthodox community philosophy is virtually confined to academia. It is the popular mysticism of Chassidism that dominates the language of virtually all Orthodox communities in non-rational terms. However, given secular philosophy's post-Wittgensteinian turmoil, the nature of God is not one of the major issues that occupy the minds of current Jewish thinkers. What does present a much greater problem is the idea of benevolence: that God rewards the good and punishes the evil and intervenes in human history.

## BENEVOLENCE

Maimonides devotes one principle to the assertion that God knows what is in the human mind. This relates to the consequential and separate principle that God rewards and punishes. This issue of whether God cares about humans and rewards them exercised Jewish minds from the very start. God repeatedly promises in the Bible that good behaviour is to be rewarded and bad behaviour punished. There seemed to be no objective criteria. Abraham asked, 'Shall the Judge of all the earth not do Justice?' Yet, as the Book of Job illustrated, forces beyond the control of man seemed to work arbitrarily. The Talmud in *Berachot 7a* asks why righteous people suffer and the wicked prosper. It offers a range of answers. An imperfect good person suffers as opposed to a perfect one. A good son of a good father does well as opposed to a good son of a bad father and vice versa. In the end the only response the Talmud seems to return to is that there is no reward in this world, only in the next.

The kabbalistic tradition comes up with an innovative solution, transmigration of souls. An innocent child must bear the soul of a previous sinner. An innocent generation suffers because it has accumulated the souls of a previous delinquent generation.

The Holocaust has presented the greatest challenge to many thinkers. In general, the Orthodox world has refused to see the Holocaust as being any different, other than in scale, to the continued oppression of Jews that is the nature of exile in the Diaspora and the result of failure to follow the ways of God during the two Temple periods. National suffering is the inevitable consequence of national failure. Some even argue that the post-Enlightenment assimilation was responsible. Others see the Holocaust as a failure of humanity, 'Where was man?' as opposed to 'Where was God?' On the one hand, it is the final proof of abandonment by God, 'God is dead'. On the other, Jewish survival proves the opposite. It is also argued that the only response must be silence in the face of such evil. A Maimonidean reply might be that one simply cannot ascribe human criteria to God, neither can we expect a non-human force to conform to human expectations. None of these arguments is specifically Jewish and they illustrate the varied nature of Jewish theological discourse.

The issue of 'good' and 'evil' is discussed in the Talmud in passing. Everything comes from God, says the Talmud. But 'everything that God does is for the best', even if we are unable to see it in that way from a human perspective. Evil does not exist as a power on its own. The Satan figure in the Book of Job acts only under the auspices of God. Isaiah says that 'God creates good and bad'. The rabbis modified this phrase when they inserted it in the morning prayers to read 'God creates everything'. Nature functions according to its own divinely ordained rules and natural catastrophes are seen as being part of that order. As for humanity, 'A person only sins when a spirit of stupidity enters him'. This is almost the equivalent of Hannah Arendt's banality of evil. Evil is what humans do.

## REVELATION

Maimonides devotes four of his principles to revelation. The words of the prophets are true, Moses was the greatest of the prophets, the Torah was revealed to Moses, and finally the Torah cannot be changed or replaced. The one that most specifically defines Judaism is the Sinai revelation that bequeathed the Torah to the Jewish people. The Mishna *Avot* opens with the words: 'Moses received the Torah on Sinai and handed it to Joshua who handed it to the Elders who passed it to the Prophets who passed it on to the Rabbis of the Great Assembly.' This line was essential in arguing that the rabbis were not innovators but transmitters of the original revelation and that the original covenant on Sinai remained in force and was not superseded by any New Testament.

Yehuda Halevy argued in the *Kuzari* that unlike all other revelations, the Jewish revelation was given in the presence of a whole nation that stood at the foot of Sinai. It was quite unlike either the Christian or the Muslim revelations that were more individual. Of course as far as other religions are concerned, regardless of what happened once, the issue became one of continuity. We need not engage with the rational validity of Halevy's argument, but it does underline the tendency to see Judaism as a religion based on national commitment as much as an individual act of faith.

When Maimonides talked about revelation, he did not mean simply the written text of the Torah, the Five Books of Moses, but also its oral traditions. The rabbinic position was that the Torah contained within it the means and the methodology of ongoing clarification and legislation. He went further and, taking his clue from the Talmud in *Sanhedrin*, argued that one could not ascribe anything in the Torah to Moses' own personal ideas or innovations. Every word was given with divine approval. Whether Maimonides believed this philosophically or not is open to debate. The Massoretic tradition fixed the accepted text of the Torah relatively late and incorporated variants in the text through the method known as the *kri ketiv*, read and written, in which some words and letters are written differently from the way they are read. Were both versions given by God? It remains an ongoing debate as to whether Maimonides wrote in two styles, that of popular education and that of more exclusive academic philosophy.

He argued that the words of the biblical prophets were also part of the revelatory process. But in neither case does he go into the exact process or explain the difference between God speaking to Moses, mouth to mouth, and the way He communicated with later prophets, other than to reiterate the supremacy of the Mosaic revelation. It is possible that he wanted to draw a very clear line between the biblical prophets and those later leaders of other religions who claimed to speaking in the name of God.

It is fair to say that this issue of revelation is one that defines an orthodox or a traditional position in Judaism. Reform and Conservative schools accept the Torah as an important expression of Jewish religious or cultural evolution and a guide to religious traditions, but not as the revealed word of God. Orthodox positions may vary in detail and even in the way they imagine the time and manner of the actual process, but all accept the superhuman element in the very inspirational nature of the Torah. It is this issue of revelation that defines sectarian Jewish identities. If the Torah in all its dimensions is divine, then the room for change is limited to the range of tools allowed for within the system. If, on the other hand, it is a human document, then, like the American Constitution there are plenty of opportunities for creative interpretation.

## MESSIANISM

The issue of Messianism remains a highly controversial one in Judaism both because of the challenge of Christianity and because of the various false Messiahs who have emerged within the tradition. The Torah uses the word for Messiah, *Mashiach*, derived from the word meaning 'to anoint with oil', to apply to a High Priest or one anointed to go with the people into battle. It is only when Samuel appoints Saul as the first king that the word is applied to a monarch. Later on anointing was only relevant when there was a break in dynasty or when there had been a challenge to succession. David is an example of the former and Solomon of the latter. This would explain why after the destruction of the Judean Kingdom, the re-establishment of the House of David would require a new king to be anointed. In this sense the Messiah is simply an anointed king. Indeed in the Book of Kings, Elijah is commanded to anoint Hazael of Aram and later Daniel refers to Cyrus, the Persian king, as God's Messiah for allowing Jews to return to their ancestral homelands. So the ceremony was not confined to Jewish kings.

Quite separately, the prophet Isaiah has visions of an era of peaceful coexistence without war and of a king reforming society, removing violence and inequity. Jewish commentators understood Isaiah's references to a leader emerging as applying to King Hezekiah, who succeeded in re-establishing Jewish religious traditions. They point out that all prophetic statements were meant to be relevant to the audience at the time and to be relatively short-term. Isaiah's predictions of the wolf lying down with the lamb are taken to be symbolic; evil or aggressive people would change and learn to get on and live in peace with the poor and the weak. The hope remained throughout the talmudic period that the natural world would change during a Messianic era. The majority opinion, however, asserted that if Isaiah was indeed looking forward to a changed world order, the only changes would be in human behaviour.

The Babylonian exiles prayed for the return of the House of David. But this was an expression of political rather than Messianic independence. The Mishna at the end of *Sotah* refers to Elijah the prophet returning to reconcile and bring peace. It also talks about the period before the Messiah arrives as being an era when the world will be so corrupt that only divine intervention will help.

The Dead Sea sects wrote about the Teacher of Righteousness who would bring peace and an end to divisions. Some might have thought that Jesus or a Jesus type might have been that figure, but Roman oppression only got worse and there was no outward sign of any change. Jews looked to a Messiah to remove Roman oppression and lead to independence. Hopes were raised by Bar Cochba in 132 CE, but then dashed. It is clear that the Jewish under-standing of Messianism in one form or another required that it would bring about a change in the world order and an end to oppression and exploitation then rather than at some later date. There is no reference in Jewish literature to a Second Coming. However, these reverses led to a restatement of the Messianic idea.

The more detailed discussion of Messianism in the Talmud *Sanhedrin* produced the following options. A minority view was that of Rabbi Hillel who declared there would not be a Messiah because all references had been to King Hezekiah. The majority foresaw a new world order, while others dreamed simply of the removal of oppression. The former had visions of fruit constantly on trees, women giving birth every day and all physical needs met so as to allow concentration on spiritual activity The less miraculously inclined simply anticipated a time when governments stopped oppression and individuals would be free to fulfil their potential.

Both groups of opinion divided again into those who believed that the Messiah would come when things got so bad they could get no worse, and those who believed that only human effort could improve the world. From this divergence developed the main conceptual alternatives in Judaism: on the one hand, the view that humans have a responsibility to improve the world and work towards a just society; on the other, the Messianic belief that God intervenes in history and will indeed do so again in order to save the world from itself.

One can well understand that during those periods of Jewish history that experienced maximum discomfort, the idea that God would intervene might have seemed the only way out. Yet under better conditions, the feeling that humans could bring about a change would have seemed more realistic. Maimonides defines the Messianic era as one in which people are freed from oppression and governmental control and are able to explore their spirituality and fulfil their potential undisturbed. Quoting one of the talmudic epigrams, he concludes that 'the only difference between life now and life under the Messiah will be governmental oppression.'

Either way, it should be clear why Jewish thinking found no room for a Messiah who failed to change anything in the physical world or restore Jewish autonomy. There are some who see the re-establishment of the State of Israel as the most positive sign since the destruction of the Temple and indeed express the idea that it is 'the first blossoming of the redemption'. The Ultra-Orthodox only accept the idea that the Messiah will be a manifestly divine intervention when the Temple will be rebuilt.

## REDEMPTION

It is worth adding within the context of Messianism, that the Hebrew words *geulah* (redemption), *hoshaa* (salvation), and other similar terms do not carry the same theological implications as they do in Christianity. As there is no sense of a fall or a state of sin, the only theological salvation in Judaism is the ability of a person to get as close to God as possible and through Teshuva (repentance) to deal with any deficiencies or failures. This is a strictly personal process that enables anyone to achieve the highest standards. The only debate has been whether, as the Mitnagdim argue, study of Torah is the primary method to achieve higher spiritual levels or, as the Chassidim and the Kabbalists argue, prayer, meditation and personal spirituality are the most effective ways. References in liturgy to salvation are restricted specifically to the removal of political and human oppression.

## AFTERLIFE

Maimonides' final principle refers to resurrection. The Torah does not specifically refer to life after death or resurrection. When describing the death of the patriarchs, it uses is the phrase, 'He became a body, died and was gathered to his people.' Given that all surrounding civilisations at the time had advanced notions of life after death and the return of the dead to life, was the absence of an explicit reference an intentional attempt to present an alternative world view, an attempt to emphasise 'this world', or simply unnecessary within the context of the Torah where such ideas would have been taken for granted? The latter is certainly the approach adopted by the rabbis who struggled to find texts that would show the resurrection was as explicit as implicit in the Torah.

## SOUL

A similar problem exists with regard to the idea of soul. If soul is a divine substance or element, then it should not be affected by the demise of a physical body. Yet the biblical words commonly associated with soul, *nefesh*, *ruach* and *neshama* are used of animals as well as humans. In the Book of Ecclesiastes the author asks, 'And who knows if the soul of a human rises and that of an animal descends?' Clearly the issue was debated even then.

The Talmud uses expressions such as the world to come, the future to come and resurrection almost interchangeably and with no clear definition or clarification. The discussion in the Talmud *Sanhedrin* does nothing to define the terms. Resurrection is elided with the world to come. Cleopatra is quoted as asking if bodies are resurrected with their clothes or naked. A rejection of the world to come is taken as being a rejection of resurrection. Resurrection itself was taken as a reference to the dead bodies the prophet Ezekiel saw in his vision in Babylon but also as a promise for the future. Both ideas were certainly part of the armoury of talmudic thought, but exactly what did they mean?

The rabbis included the expression 'reviving the dead' in the daily liturgy, but they also used the expression to refer to the power of rain to bring life to nature. Why did they select this expression and not 'life after death'?

In his '*Guide*' Maimonides does not refer to resurrection at all. He talks only about the continuity of the soul and life after death. As a result he was accused of heresy and had to publish a special pamphlet justifying himself. He said that he did indeed believe in resurrection but could neither explain it nor say very much about it. It is almost as though he was arguing that what was required by the idea was the acceptance of God's capacity to do anything. Again the question was whether he was saying one thing to the rationalists and another to the popular community. In his *Principles* he only mentions resurrection as a required belief and does not talk about the afterlife at all. A strange omission unless the two are synonymous.

## HEAVEN AND HELL

What is meant by heaven (or the Garden of Eden) and hell is open to a range of different interpretations. The Talmud has large numbers of quotations about the delight that awaits the righteous in the world to come. The imagery is one of dwelling in the presence of God and of eternal pleasure from this proximity. The nearest one gets to a physical description is that of the Garden of Eden, but even then nowhere is a list of physical pleasures described. The Talmud quotes: 'In the world to come there is no eating or drinking or other pleasure, only the good will sit with crowns on their heads delighting in the presence of God.'

Hell, *gehenna*, derived from Gey Hinnom, also borrows a biblical simile named after a valley outside Jerusalem where children were passed through fire in acts of pagan worship. Maimonides argues that hell is simply physical death, which happens to anyone whose behaviour on earth has eradicated the spiritual dimension of a person, whereas heaven is simply the reunification of the soul with its maker. Nevertheless, popular tradition preserved these ideas in a far more vivid form than the philosophers were prepared to tolerate. The idea that the soul progresses from body to heaven through various stages and hurdles continues to find expression in the language and rituals of mourning. This gives it an important place in the psyche of Jews. The popular and the academic theological strands coexisted in Judaism as much as in any other religious culture.

The result is that traditionally these concepts have come to be accepted by the vast majority of practising Jews without question. The Talmud, the *Zohar* and other main books of Kabbalah take these ideas at face value and there is no serious debate of these concepts nowadays in talmudic academies. In day-to-day Jewish life these issues do not arise. There is no call to pronounce a credo other than the Shema and the issue arises only in Orthodox circles if it is challenged. It seems that the rabbis of the Talmud and their successors worried mainly about atheists rather than agnostics. Their concern was that spirituality accepts any divine possibility and transcends the restrictions of the physical. Limiting God or what might happen was seen as a deficiency in trust. The Hebrew word for 'belief', *emunah*, really means 'trust' and 'confidence', rather than an intellectual assertion of the reality of life.

Reform and its allied movements do not feel in anyway bound by the theological agenda of Maimonides nor indeed of the Talmud, whereas the Ultra-Orthodox world is simply not interested in engaging with a theological mindset that is perceived as being alien and antithetic to Jewish values.

## DETERMINISM VERSUS FREE WILL

The sort of debate that Ultra-Orthodox Judaism engages in concerns the difference between what is called fate, or determinism, and free will and the freedom to act. Based entirely on talmudic sources, the issue is the extent to which external forces, angels, *mazal* (astrology), spirits and the spiritual world control our lives.

Maimonides, the rationalist, rejected all such notions as being the result of a credulous age, despite the frequency of supporting sources in the Talmud. The term mazal is used only late in the Bible with regard to the signs of the Zodiac. Given the almost universal interest in astrology, it is hardly surprising that Jews found it attractive despite the repeated imprecations against any form of divining in the Torah. The Talmud quotes the view that 'Mazal controls how much money one makes, how long one lives and how many children one has'; but this is countered by the view that 'Everything is in the hands of God except fear of God', or its variant 'Everything is in the hands of God except traps and colds' (what happens when you do not take care).

Mazal developed into a more general term that recognised that heavenly bodies did indeed exert some influence on matters on earth and from this extended to all those areas where external factors influenced individual human affairs.

The frequent use of the word 'angel' in the Torah is balanced by the fact that no specific name is given for an angel, which in Hebrew is defined using exactly the same word as 'messenger'. All angel-messengers are seen as acting simply as agents of divine will. Miracles, despite their frequency in the Torah, are downgraded as being secondary vehicles of communication. According to Maimonides, they are only for those of 'little belief'.

The frequency of miracles during the Exodus does not seem to have helped reinforce faith very much. Indeed in Deuteronomy chapter 13, a false prophet is described as someone who has miraculous powers and can foretell the future but whose message is a betrayal of the revealed Torah. It is the text that counts far more than wonders of any sort given the possibilities for abuse (as illustrated by the Egyptian magicians who could replicate some of Moses' miracles). The Talmud warns against relying on miracles and exhorts people to take control of their own lives.

An issue such as whether God, knowing everything, limits human action is not raised in talmudic thinking. Maimonides resolves the problem by asserting that God has given humans choices and free will and that his fore-knowledge, since it is confined to the realms of the divine, has no bearing on human actions. Yet in common Orthodox parlance today everything, from one's marriage partner to one's career, is seen as being divinely ordained, although good behaviour can have an impact on that decision.

The kabbalistic system of angelology and detailed astrological influence has over time come to exert a more powerful influence on Jewish life than the rational. The reaction against modernity within the Orthodox world has led to a mistrust of rationalism.

## HUMAN RIGHTS

There is no statement of human rights in the Torah, only obligations. Yet the importance of human rights in our modern societies does present a challenge to religious thinkers. If the revealed law is absolute, then how can any external system of values be acceptable?

One of the responses is that Jewish law can under certain circumstances be overruled. In a situation of life and death Jews may transgress all Torah laws except for three. They may not blaspheme against God, kill an innocent third party, or commit adultery. The whole system of Jewish law is predicated on the opinion of an expert. Faced with difficult situations the halachic expert may find grounds for leniency in one situation and rigidity in another, even though on the surface the problem is the same and the guidelines for dealing with it do not change. This is why meta-halachic phrases are repeated throughout the Torah, 'Do Justice', 'Do that which is good and right', whereas it might have been enough to say simply 'Obey the Law'.

External factors can be taken into consideration. The need to live on good terms with others, public opinion, and behaving in an outwardly acceptable manner all figure within halachic debates. Precisely because the human element is such an important one in the exposition of Jewish law, it is argued that it is only right and proper to come to terms with other systems of justice and morality so long as they are predicated on an ethical basis that conforms to the seven Noachide principles.

In modern societies that are no longer based entirely on religious values other values have developed. Jewish law specifies the responsibilities of children towards their parents and parents towards their children. But rights are a new development. Jews are expected to abide by the law of the land.

In matters of sexuality traditional laws are out of tune with current ones. How is a Jew to respond? Not by abandoning the traditional values, but by adopting additional ones of tolerance. How does one decide which of these to adopt? In the case of women's rights the issue goes further. Should not rabbis take on board new considerations in the way they deal with women, given an inevitable bias in a system administered by males?

Prevailing opinion in the Charedi camp is to ignore the issue. In the wider traditional camp it is to seek some accommodation. In the Reform world it is to accept current attitudes over traditional Jewish ones.

## A JUST WAR

Another issue that has become an actuality is that of a just war. There is no such concept in the Torah. There are two categories of war, a *Milchemet Mitzvah* (an obligatory war) and a *Milchemet Reshut* (an optional war). The Milchemet Mitzvah applies only to self-defence. In biblical times it also applied to the seven Canaanite tribes, but this has been inoperative for nearly 3,000 years. Self-defence is an important biblical principle. It is raised in the context of killing an intruder. The idea of turning the other cheek is to be found in Judaism only with regard to personal behaviour in non-legislative or physical situations. Otherwise, all steps taken to defend oneself against an aggressor are allowed in proportion to the danger.

The optional war required a whole set of circumstances that are no longer applicable. It required the approval of the Sanhedrin and the High Priesthood consulting the twelve stones on the breastplate known as the *Urim* and *Thumim*. These were a sort of oracle or auspices that existed at the time of the first Temple but were then lost and not replaced. The whole framework for optional wars has fallen into abeyance and cannot be used as a halachic category anymore. Self-defence is the only option left. The Torah avoids suggesting that it is good or just. Rather, it is a sad necessity.

## AESTHETICS

The Christian, Hindu and Buddhist religions have a long tradition of encouraging religious art. Judaism, as with Islam, is strongly opposed to representational art in its places of worship. How far can this be said to reflect an antipathy to the arts?

The Ten Commandments forbade making any images of anything in the material world. However, the qualification given was that they should not be made as objects of worship. The Talmud records that in order to determine the calendar by visual sightings of the moon, the rabbis used to keep models of the heavens and the celestial bodies for demonstration purposes. Excavations in Galilee show that there were mosaics around the walls and floors of synagogues 2,000 years ago and the craftsmanship that began with Bezalel's construction of the Tabernacle continued in the Temple, and in general craftsmanship was highly valued and appreciated throughout the two Jewish Commonwealths.

One suspects that the clash with Greek civilisation began to affect attitudes. Although Jewish priests were in the forefront of introducing Greek sports and buildings into Jerusalem, grass-roots opposition opposed any signs or symbols of Greek culture. The pious Jews considered the naked human form, so beloved of the new civilisation, immodest. To make matters worse, the attempt to place effigies of rulers in the Temple led to open rebellion in the case of Antiochus IV.

The association of Christianity with Greek culture over time perpetuated this antipathy. The statues that changed from being of Greek gods and goddesses to Christian deities were behind the decision to introduce a complete ban on the human form in three dimensions.

Jews living in Islamic societies continued with their artistic professions and creativity. Islam, too, banned human representation and in its mosques only colours, patterns and wording were used for decoration. Jews excelled as silver and goldsmiths, making religious objects and artefacts that the wealthy commissioned and used in pursuit of the religious command to glorify God. This command was used to encourage the appreciation of and investment in objects of beauty and skill.

In Christian societies non-Christians were not allowed to join guilds so that craftsmanship amongst Jews in Europe during the medieval period was lost. The decorations on early manuscripts (most notably the Passover *Haggadot*) were all made by non-Jewish artists. Often they were stylised representations of Christian saints and knights transposed onto a Jewish liturgical text.

So it would be inaccurate to say that Judaism does not appreciate or encourage the aesthetic. In the context of modern Jewish law an artist has great freedom provided he or she is not making the work in order for it to be worshipped. Some religious artists are stricter and make sure that their human representations are never complete. But in this modern era of non-representational art that is hardly a problem.

## MISSION

The idea of mission is essential in Christianity but not in Judaism. The main reason is that Judaism has not adopted the position that everyone has to be saved and that there is only one route to God. This does not mean that Jews do not believe that their religion is divinely ordained or 'true', but that there are different paths and ways of expressing one's relation with God. It would be fair to say that there are 'truths'. The way of life expected of a priest in Temple times, or the symbolic way priests are still called first to read from the Torah, was different to that of an ordinary Jew. Women have a different set of obligations to men, but no one has ever suggested that either are in any way inferior religiously or inadequate. The covenant Jews have with God imposes different sets of obligations.

Judaism does strongly insist on the equivalent of 'witness'. In Hebrew the term is *Kiddush HaSHem* (sanctifying the divine name). Maimonides mentions this as the primary objective of all Jews and lists it as the first obligation in his work on Jewish law. Sanctifying God's name involves behaving in a way that brings credit to one as a human being and as a Jew. Behaviour that brings odium or leads people to disrespect Jews is regarded as *Chillul HaShem* (desecrating God's name). Notice that these terms talk about sanctifying or desecrating God's name not the name of a human. If God ordains a Jew's behaviour and if that behaviour is not God-like, then this leads inevitably to one questioning divine revelation.

The Talmud is so insistent on this that it declares that someone who desecrates the name of God cannot derive any consolation from the Day of Atonement. Sadly, as in any community, there are those who often fail to live up to their ideals. But as the Mishna says, 'If a person is well regarded by other human beings this is a sign that he is well regarded by God', and the reverse holds true as well.

There is debate over the mission of the Jews to the nations of the world. If the idea of a 'chosen people' is one of responsibility to 'improve the world', *tikkun olam* in Hebrew, then it is argued that Jews have to be more proactive in spreading their message. Against this it is argued that the non-Jewish world only needs to adhere to the basic seven Noachide commandments and virtually all religions now meet these requirements. The preoccupation of the Jews has become one of survival rather than mission.

## RACE, RELIGION OR NATION

There is no hint anywhere in Jewish sources of a distinction based on race. Judaism requires adherence to its principles, but anyone, regardless of race, can accept these and become a part of the Jewish people. A visit to Israel today will reveal a complete racial spectrum of practising Jews.

The Bible talks about a nation, a people: AM, rather like the Muslim UMMA. However this designation does not mean that Judaism does not see itself as having a universal role. The idea of a Jewish nation is an extension of the idea of a family: a group of people sharing common ties and ways of living provide support and example. Love of Israel, extolled throughout the liturgy, is the love of those who share spiritual and ethical values, as well as those who have formally accepted a specific code. If peoples currently express themselves through nationalism, Judaism too has the right to its own national home, but the Messianic ideal would be the removal of national barriers and a universe of tolerance and co-operation.

The word 'religion' does not feature in the Bible. If religion is defined as a system of beliefs then Judaism may well fail the test because behaviour counts far more than commitment to a particular credo (which in itself is a controversial issue in Judaism). Similarly, 'faith community', although correct in that certain ideas and beliefs are shared, is less accurate than to describe Judaism as a way of life, a divinely ordained programme for making the most of the world we find ourselves in.

# Chapter 8

# Judaism Today

The Jewish people today number approximately twelve million. Given that 2,000 years ago, most experts calculate that Jews accounted for more than ten per cent of the Roman Empire and double that in Babylon, this represents a massive decline. Nevertheless, it is true to say that Judaism as an intensely practised religion is growing in strength and has come back from the brink of extinction that the Nazi Holocaust almost achieved.

Jews are centred predominantly in Israel and North America. Other major communities exist in Russia, France and Britain, and to a lesser extent throughout Europe and in parts of Africa, South America, the Far East and Australasia.

Jews tend to be able to recognise each other by their appearance, country of origin and behavioural patterns. For example, a French Jew's pronunciation of Hebrew immediately marks him or her out from an American Jew, a Muscovite Jew's pronunciation from an Azerbaijani Jew, and so on. Were it not for a common religious code of behaviour that links the daily life and religious rituals of such disparate people, each would probably feel more at home with people of the same nationality, which is very often the case, and only anti-Semitism forces these disparate Jews together.

Most Jews today do not follow the Jewish religion very strictly. Amongst those who do, on a purely religious level, it is simplistic but handy to describe the committed by their headgear. The Reform and Conservative communities, in general, do not wear specifically Jewish garments. If they cover their heads at all, it will be very occasionally, at home on festive occasions, or in the synagogue.

Some Conservative and Modern Orthodox Jews will cover their heads with small cappels of varying size and colour. However many, at work and in society in general do not wear religious headgear except for religious occasions. The Ultra-Orthodox world now prefers to call itself *Charedi*. This derives from the biblical expression 'to tremble before God'. The Charedi community wear black hats and, in addition, their relaxed informal headgear is the black cappel. Within each of these categories there are varying theological, geographic, sectarian and political variations. Indeed, within the Charedi world you can tell which Chassidic group or yeshiva a person belongs to by the shape and size of his black hat. Some of these sects will speak to members of different sects, while others will not. So the unwary outsider is often guilty of solecism by grouping Jews together. Every community of Jews defies absolute categories. Just as some Christians and Muslims use internal religious differences not to talk to others if they can avoid it, so too, sadly, this is the case within Judaism. Sometimes only a common external threat forces Jews into communication.

## JUDAISM IN ISRAEL

The Jews of Israel today are the most varied and numerous of all Jewish communities. But they live in an atmosphere of tension not just because of the external political situation but also because of the conflicting elements that helped create the state.

There was constant tension between the various secular branches of Zionism, some more radical or more socialist than others, and the right-wing secular 'Revisionists', the body of Zionists loyal to Vladimir Jabotinsky. This division was mirrored by the tension among 'the Old *Yishuv*', the Orthodox communities that had existed on charitable support, who refused to have anything to do with the godless new immigrants that the Zionist movement was bringing to Israel, or indeed even with the religious Zionists.

A small group of religious leaders, however, did encourage the new settlers. Men like the great first Chief Rabbi of Israel under the British Mandate, Rabbi Kook, saw them as divine agents. Before the Second World War the religious leadership of Eastern Europe had refused to encourage emigration to Israel. As a result the majority of the founders and settlers of the new State were secular and had every reason to expect that it would indeed become a secular state.

### State and Religion

After the establishment of the State in 1948 the founding Prime Minister Ben Gurion had to reconcile two parties. On the one hand, he had to deal with the right-wing secular parties, heirs to the Jabotinsky tradition headed by Menachem Begin. Ben Gurion had to head off a potential civil war between rival militias. He also had to deal with religious communities of various hues who had a great deal of support outside Israel.

The majority of the religious communities (at the time, the minute anti-Zionist Charedi Neturei Karta party alone refused any co-operation) decided to enter the political process, and the tradition of political bargaining, in which the demands of one group were met to offset the challenge from another, set the tone for Israeli political and religious life. Religious parties agreed to vote with Ben Gurion provided that he met certain conditions that would guarantee the Jewish character of the new State.

The agreement meant that Israel would have two legal systems, the civil one based on a combination of Ottoman, Mandate and Jewish law, interacting with the Knesset (parliament) and the Supreme Court. The religious system with its own judges and courts would coexist as an optional alternative. All marriages and burials would be carried out solely by the religious authorities. Other religions would be entitled to their own rites and to manage their own affairs. Shabbat, as the seventh day, would be the official day of rest and festivals observed by Government offices and it was left to local authorities to negotiate the extent to which services and economic activities would be allowed on that day.

## The Law of Return

The State had ceded matters of personal status to the religious authorities. Yet the 'Law of Return' was defined by a secular Knesset to allow anyone claiming one Jewish grandparent to obtain automatic citizenship in Israel. Never again would someone persecuted for being Jewish be defenceless because there was no state to defend them. This was a reaction to Hitler's definition of a Jew rather than the traditional halachic definition, which is the child of a Jewish mother. This created an ongoing battle over Jewish status. Jews who had abandoned Judaism for another religion remained Jewish halachically but were not recognised under the Law of Return, whilst converts to Judaism in Reform communities were excluded because religious definitions in Israel were exclusively halachic. This issue has continued to create problems as each new wave of immigration, whether from Ethiopia or Russia, brings in new citizens who become Israelis and yet are either not always recognised religiously as Jews, or indeed are practising Christians.

This agreement set the tone for a major division within Israel. The secular Jews have always objected to religious coercion, particularly when it is seen as a tool of political bargaining. The Orthodox and Charedi Jews object to secular interference in religious affairs. One of the most negative by-products of this process is that the religious parties enter into negotiations from as extreme a position as possible knowing that they will have to compromise. Religious issues therefore are always presented in an extreme form and this both militates against modernity and presents a negative image of the Charedi world in Israel.

## Conscription

The issue of conscription is a good illustration. Ben Gurion was persuaded that the Holocaust had seriously degraded Jewish religious scholarship and he agreed to give yeshiva students exemption from military service to concentrate on their studies. The Modern Orthodox Jews did not take advantage of this and, on the contrary, made a point of combining study with military service. But the Charedi world treated study and exemption as the norm. At the time the number involved was barely 500 a year. Nowadays the number has grown to almost 50,000.

All attempts to modify the arrangement have failed. The religious position is that prayer and study also play a part in the struggle for survival. How, they argue, is one to evaluate the success of military might over divine intervention? Yet the vast majority of the exemptions nowadays go to young men who neither study nor pray very much and simply use this as an excuse for avoiding military service. Since such exemptions are conditional on not working, vast numbers of able-bodied men do nothing and are dependent on social welfare or on their wives working for them. In the Fifties some in the Charedi world were prepared to compromise and send the less academic young men into the army. But over the years the bargaining position has hardened and even some form of National Guard or welfare service has been rejected on the grounds that this would be the thin edge of the wedge. This reluctance has caused deep offence and divisions. Many parents see their children killed in defence of their land while Charedi youngsters live a life dependent on state welfare, yet refuse to serve. Men who have served are expected to go on doing reservist duty throughout their active lives, but Charedi men are exempt (as indeed are Arab citizens).

## Religious Nationalism

The Charedi world continues to expand on the basis of a very high birth rate and very low attrition. Its position in the political life of Israel is gaining strength rather than weakening. Similarly the Modern Orthodox Jewish communities of Israel have expanded, particularly in the post-1967 period. The religious Zionist movements found themselves caught between the secular pioneers on one side and the pious religious on the other. After 1967 it was the religious Zionists who spearheaded the expansion into the West Bank territories as acts of religious pioneering. This new Charedi *Leumi*, nationalist extremism, gave them a new lease of life. It was they, rather than the Charedi communities, who fought for the land and refused to give up one inch on religious grounds.

The Charedi world had always argued for concessions in the interest of peace. Charedi communities moved into the West Bank simply for economic reasons, cheap accommodation. The religious Zionists moved for ideological reasons. This political shift of religious Zionism to the right has had a significant impact on the flagship academic institution of religious Zionism, the Bar Ilan University outside Tel Aviv. At one stage a significant part of its student body was much influenced by the sort of ideology that bred the assassination of the Israeli Prime Minister Yitschak Rabin. Fortunately there has been a reaction away from this extremism.

## Sepharadi and Ashkenazi

There is one other important factor needed to understand the complexion of religious life in Israel today. The Eastern European Jews considered themselves and their values to be superior to those of either the religious or the oriental communities. As a result, when Jews were expelled from Arab countries after 1948 and came to Israel they were not treated with sufficient respect by the secular Israeli establishment. They were made to feel that their loyalty to tradition was outdated and primitive. This bred resentment. Slowly, as the oriental communities established themselves in Israel, they began to exert their own political influence.

In the late Seventies the Sepharadim were responsible for the change in power that ejected the old Mapai left-wing hierarchy, which had governed Israel for the first twenty-five years, in favour of Menachem Begin and his right-wing alliance. But they re-established their own brand of religiosity, which was in some ways more simply traditional and in others more flexible and tolerant than the norms that characterised the European religious communities.

As a result today a greater proportion of Israelis are traditionally inclined, even though many of them are not at all comfortable with the political position of religious parties and prefer to vote for secular parties.

The secular communities are divided into those who are anti-religious on principle and opposed to state and religion being intertwined; and those who are interested in spirituality but are offended by the established rabbinate and religious coercion and look elsewhere for their religious inspiration. Then there are those secular Jews who support religious institutions out of a feeling of guilt combined with the conviction that only extremists can keep the religion alive. Into this eastern maelstrom the Reform movements of the West have tried very hard to make inroads, but so far with only limited success.

Yet despite the seeming chaos, religious life in Israel is far more productive and creative than anywhere else. There have never been so many religious schools, seminaries, colleges and centres of full-time adult study and research, so many centres of religious experiment, spiritual concentration, outreach and innovation as there are today in Israel of almost every complexion.

Outreach centres that train teachers and rabbis to go out into the world to bring Jews back to the faith have blossomed in recent years and exercise a significant influence on Diaspora communities. All of this is thanks both to private and state funding. There have never been so many universities with thriving Jewish study departments producing so much scholarship as there are today in Israel. Indeed, innovative religious thinking in Judaism is nowadays almost entirely confined to academia.

## Secular Judaism

One might have expected secular Judaism to develop a strong alternative to traditional religious expressions. At the moment no such movement has achieved any serious degree of success. There are individuals of talent and ability who argue for an alternative expression of Jewish tradition. Successful centres for teaching traditional texts in non-traditional ways have flourished, but so far no real alternative to long-established traditions has yet emerged. Perhaps the massive Russian immigration of an overwhelmingly non-Jewish character may change this. As elsewhere in the world, apathy characterises the non-religious world more than creative opposition.

Significant numbers, mainly of secular Israelis, have left Israel over the past fifty years. It is estimated that nearly a million Israelis have moved, mainly to the United States of America, since Israeli Independence. In general, they are more likely to integrate into the dominant culture than into the local Jewish communities. Religious Israelis who migrate on the other hand, all find their places and contribute significantly to the host Jewish communities.

## New Legal Challenges

Jewish religious law was for centuries confined to ritual or abstraction. Today it has to deal with the political, industrial, scientific, medical, agricultural and ethical issues that the very nature of being part of the governance of a modern state demands. Works of Jewish law are rolling off the presses as never before. As a result almost every Diaspora community now relies on Israel for manpower, technical law and educational support. Most Diaspora rabbis study in Israel and hardly a Jewish school of any colour in the Diaspora survives without input from Israel.

Although it is true that some of the fastest growing Chassidic communities around the world still maintain an anti-Zionist stance, they all have strong presences in Israel and benefit from the advantages of a Jewish State and the inevitable flow of human beings and material that enriches the Diaspora communities. However great some Diaspora religious academies are, they all come second now to Israel in terms of richness and depth of scholarship. Religious life in Israel is, despite the tensions, more vibrant and creative than it has probably ever been since the destruction of the Temple.

## THE DIASPORA

In the Diaspora itself there are quite different forces at work. Assimilation remains the major issue with estimates of approximately fifty per cent of all Jews marrying out of the religion or abandoning their Jewish identity. And yet the picture is not quite as negative as it seems. Ben Gurion had believed that the Diaspora was doomed to extinction. Many Zionists believed ideologically that one should do nothing to support the continuity of Diaspora communities. But over time the realisation that the Diaspora was a potential ally and support, and the intermingling of Israeli and Diaspora communities, has changed this absolutist perception

## Jewish Education

One of the factors that has revived the Diaspora has been Jewish education. There was a time when most Jews disregarded the importance of Jewish education. They thought that the best way to succeed in the Diaspora was to become as similar to the host nation as possible. They tended to prefer to send their children to state or private schools.

This is no longer the case for several reasons. The collapse of standards in much of state education has turned Jewish education into an attractive alternative. Graduates of Jewish schools have shown themselves just as capable of succeeding academically, professionally and socially as graduates of other schools. A desire to keep Judaism alive has led to the realisation that only a good Jewish education can really help turn the tide (although it is a moot point as to whether school or home exercises the greater influence). Jewish education has expanded exponentially. Even sections of Judaism previously opposed to the idea, such as Reform Judaism, are now beginning to see the benefits.

Jews in the Diaspora are now less insecure and apologetic. They are more inclined to fight for their rights and this includes demanding state support for Jewish education in those countries that do offer subsidies to denominational education. Interestingly, the Charedi communities tend to fight shy of state support because this often comes with demands for standards of secular education they are reluctant to accept.

## The Religious Right

The most remarkable phenomenon of Diaspora Jewry has been the almost universal and amazing resurgence of the Charedi world and the parallel expansion of Charedi outreach to the assimilating Jewish world. It is true to say that the middle ground of most Jewish communities is being polarised. Whilst the majority are moving away from Judaism altogether, a sizeable minority is moving to a much more intensive expression of their Judaism. The result is that the rabbinate in the Modern Orthodox centres of Europe and America are becoming increasingly Charedi in outlook and loyalty. Articulate and energetic, they are setting the agenda for Jewish communities and even rivalling the Reform rabbinate in the areas of public debate, interaction with society and communication.

The Charedi tendencies of Diaspora communities have meant that theological debate and innovation are discouraged and conformity plays a greater role in religious communities than spirituality. Similarly, the Charedi disdain for Reform and other progressive movements means that they refuse to recognise or co-operate with them. In many respects they would be happier dealing with non-Jews than with other Jews they consider to be undermining their religious position.

In England and America even the centrist Modern Orthodox refuse to work with Reform communities on religious, as opposed to social, issues. This has been exacerbated by the patrilineal issue whereby Reform recognises the children of non-Jewish fathers, Reform conversions, seen by the Orthodox as too lenient, and Reform attitudes to marriage and divorce. Orthodoxy does not accept religious ceremonies carried out by those who themselves do not lead an Orthodox life. In practice this has led to such a schism that the two communities effectively have all but become two religions within one nation. The drift of the centre to the right has made this split even greater.

In this respect Judaism is experiencing a similar movement to that discernable in Christianity, Islam and all the major world religions. The perception is that secular society has failed and the scientific revolution has not addressed ethical and spiritual issues. This has led to a significant rise of interest in these areas and in lifestyle solutions to the pressures of modern living. Established religious structures are perceived to be too preoccupied with power and authority, leading to compromise and a wishy-washy approach to religious commitment. Hence those movements that offer passion, commitment, personal engagement and a greater degree of individual religious responsibility are succeeding where others are not.

## UNITED STATES

### Reform and Conservative Jewry

Although the Reform movement started in Europe, it is in America where it has become the strongest denomination numerically. Next in pure size comes the more recent, more traditional, Conservative movement. Originally they felt that their alternative to traditional Judaism would sweep the board in the New World. It was less demanding ritually and much more open intellectually, and it was seen as a progressive force focusing on Judaism's moral and ethical message. Not only has this not happened but also Reform itself has turned markedly back towards tradition. Those Jews who are active members of the Reform and particularly the Conservative movement (also known as *Masorti* in some countries) today tend to have a greater degree of knowledge and commitment than their predecessors. They still remain, numerically, the largest denominations of Jews in America together with alternative religious ideologies that America spawned, such as Reconstructionism or New Age expressions of a more spiritual and less structured Judaism. They have provided a safety net for Jews wanting a lesser degree of religious commitment on the one hand, and for those wishing to join Judaism but at a simpler level of obligation on the other.

American Jewish public life, during the past two centuries, has been dominated by Reform and Conservative Jews. The leadership of most American Jewish communal organisations has been non-Orthodox. Most of the wealth of the community has been in non-Orthodox hands. Each denomination has its own academic and rabbinic institutions: the Hebrew Union College of Cincinnati, the Jewish Theological Society and the Yeshiva University. Important as they are, they are being challenged by Israeli institutions, by a range of other smaller but significant institutions, and in addition by many universities which have significant departments of Jewish Studies. The big Jewish institutions no longer dominate in the way they used to.

Fifty years ago the crystal-ball readers would have predicted that American Jewry would come to dominate Jewish life. Numerically, it is indeed by far the largest Jewish community. It is constantly being added to by immigration from all other Jewish communities attracted by the American dream and a violence-free way of life, particularly from Israel. Politically, American Jewry, on the back of the most powerful nation, does indeed exert influence not only on Israel but also on Europe, and is active in support of Jews throughout the world. The extent to which it influences American policy is arguable. It is a very small minority. Many American Jews are highly assimilated and are often more critical of Judaism and Israel than most opponents. Nevertheless, American Jewry is struggling to sustain itself in an open society and is losing membership both through assimilation and marriage out at a frightening rate.

The important feature of American Jewry is the comfort that Jews feel in a society where class, prejudice and anti-Semitism (although still to be found) no longer make Jews eager to escape their roots. In most areas of American society and culture Jews flourish. However, this is a social rather than a religious phenomenon. The phenomenal success of Jews in the areas of literature, theatre and academe has had an impact on general American life but hardly at all on Judaism as a religion. Here the rise of the Charedi world is, as elsewhere, the most interesting feature as Orthodoxy comes back from the brink of extinction to play an increasingly dominant role in American Jewish life.

## The Impact of the Holocaust

The Holocaust has also had a major impact on Jewish life in America. Initially it was largely ignored. Many of the post-war immigrants who had survived and come to America, just wanted to forget their experiences. For many Americans what happened in Europe was remote. It had to do with a continent they wanted to leave behind.

Since the Sixties this has changed. Books about the Holocaust started to appear and the issue emerged from the conspiracy of silence or neglect it had suffered from. The discussion of what happened has made Americans aware of the importance of the wider Jewish world. Questions of whether American Jewry did enough to rescue the European Jews have become a major issue.

Throughout the United States Holocaust studies have mushroomed. In many cases this is as much to do with studying the phenomenon of racism as it is do with the specific Jewish experience. However, the Holocaust has become a cause that has enabled Jews to identify without having to adopt religious practices. The establishment of Holocaust memorials in Washington, New York and Los Angeles has helped to foster an interest in the Holocaust. An 'industry' has mushroomed based on recalling personal experiences before the generation that suffered dies out and writing about this horrific phenomenon in human history.

In one way this has indeed led to a determination to fight harder against racism. Sadly, the great enthusiasm that Reform Jewry had for civil rights has now been affected by increasing black anti-Semitism and a mood of inward-looking self-preservation has become prevalent. Whereas assimilated Jews have retained a balanced and even left-wing perception of the Israel-Palestinian conflict, the Orthodox and other committed communities have become increasingly aggressive in their absolutism. The fight for survival in cultural terms has been allied to the fight for survival in Israel and has created a new and different kind of American Jewish community.

## America and Israel

American Jewry has an increasing Israeli element, so many Israelis have emigrated from Israel to the United States since 1948. Many Israeli Americans continue to have family ties with Israel and this also affects American Jewish life, even though many of the Israeli emigrants assimilate quickly into non-Jewish American life. Whereas many earlier immigrants gravitated towards synagogues and religious communities, many Israelis avoid any contact with Jewish communities when they first come. They bring with them the antipathy towards clericalism prevalent in secular Israeli society. It is only later, when they come to realise the nature of the role that religious communities play in America, that they too often find their way back into Jewish life. Similarly, large numbers of Russian Jewish immigrants are belatedly establishing contact with Jewish communities in America. Increasingly the religious movements are the ones that reach out to these communities and offer religious and social support to them.

Another feature of American Jewish life is the increasing tendency for American Jewry to move from a left-wing Democratic position towards Republicanism. Many of the Eastern European immigrants brought with them their left-wing attitudes. But as Jews become more upwardly mobile, they have tended to move politically to the right. The Charedi Jews have allied themselves with the religious right because they share certain agendas, such as supporting vouchers for private education and opposition to lenient abortion and contraceptive laws. Furthermore, the Evangelical support for Israel has brought about increasing ties between unlikely allies.

## Canada

Much of what applies to America is also true of Canada except that it has always been more traditional and conservative. Canada retains something of the English reserve inherited from its Commonwealth roots. Toronto is its largest and most impressive centre with a range of denominations and well-established educational and communal organisations. In many ways it is the perfect paradigm of the adaptability of Old World Judaism to the Modern.

## Southern America

Central and Southern America, too, have important Jewish centres, particularly in Mexico and Argentina. They were a combination of early Spanish immigrants and then Yiddish-speaking émigrés from Europe. They retain a strong secular Jewish culture. But they too are satellites and increasingly turn towards North America or Israel for survival.

## WESTERN EUROPE

The French Jewish community is the largest in Europe. Today it is made up predominantly of Jews from North Africa and has a Sepharadi character. This is augmented by the Chassidic Lubavitch movement, which has always had an educational presence and influence in Morocco. As a result many Lubavitch North African rabbis have been influential in sustaining Jewish life in France. The old Ashkenazi communities have shrunk significantly and their presence is felt more in the secular intellectual input of French Jewry. In many respects, French Jewry is intellectually creative in a remarkable way. The impact of men like Levinas who combine philosophy with Jewish source material has been greater in academia than in Jewish religious communities. But the nature of French particularism has prevented French Jewry from having much of an impact beyond its own borders. The rise in power and influence of French Muslims and their new proactive political activity has sadly led to a significant increase in the feeling of insecurity amongst many French Jews. Emigration to Israel has increased significantly and outward signs of Jewishness are now discouraged. The current mood of French Jewry is not upbeat.

Anglo-Jewry has declined steadily since the Second World War both because of emigration and assimilation. It lies in the shadow of Israel and America both in terms of its institutions and its leadership. The United Synagogue, the mainstream religious organisation that is based on the Church of England, which has dominated religious life since Victorian times, has lost out to more dynamic movements both to the left and the right of the religious spectrum. It has no strong intellectual academic tradition like its American, Israeli or even French counterparts. Of course, it is unfair to compare a community of barely 250,000 to ones of a million and upwards. But Anglo-Jewry has taken on the characteristics of its host community. It thinks of itself still as a major influence and retains the conservative British reserve that inhibits innovation. Most of the creative aspects of Jewish life, and there plenty of them, have come from outside the Establishment and usually despite it. In Britain too the growing, aggressive Charedi communities have begun to exercise a polarising influence on Jewish life and there is little exchange between the denominations.

Despite the feeling that anti-Semitism has increased, Anglo-Jewry is overwhelmingly well integrated, confident and secure. It too is conscious that there are well over ten times as many Muslims as Jews and that it will need to fight to preserve its position. But there is a feeling that extremism is less of a threat in Britain than in France or Belgium.

Emigration from the former Soviet republics has had a significant influence on the German Jewish community, which is also increasing in numbers. Germany has, ironically, always had a strong community of Israelis. But its institutions are small and beleaguered. Holland, Italy, Switzerland, Austria, Spain and Scandinavia are small communities, offering Jewish religious facilities and struggling to retain their younger generations, which gravitate towards larger centres. But here too small communities are split between the various denominations. As the saying goes, wherever you have two Jews you have two synagogues.

Only Antwerp in Belgium, of the smaller nations, is a strong vibrant community, probably percentage-wise the most Charedi community in the world. But it is small, numbering about 15,000. Brussels too has a Jewish community and one with a significant secular element. Belgium Jewry has also begun to feel Islamic pressure. Several significant rabbis have been attacked by Muslim extremists in recent years. Emigration to Israel is an increasing feature of Belgian Jewish life.

## RUSSIA AND THE FORMER SOVIET REPUBLICS

Since the collapse of the Soviet Union, the Jewish communities have begun to experience something of a revival. Initially anyone with a spark of Jewish interest went to Israel. In particular, Jews from the Caucasus and the South Eastern States had retained a stronger form of Jewish identity and joined many of their relatives already in Israel. Subsequently, large numbers of Russians with very faint Jewish connections if at all, many members of the Russian Orthodox Church, emigrated more for economic reasons.

In recent years some of these immigrants have returned to Russia. Some returned for economic or security reasons and others in order to teach and help re-establish religious institutions throughout the Old Russian empire.

The Chassidic Lubavitch movement was founded in Russia and had always maintained contacts during the darkest Stalinist eras. After Gorbachev it was well placed to expand and flourish and has, in effect, become the major Jewish influence now in the former Soviet republics, effectively challenging the original 'official' communities maintained by the Soviet government. But Reform communities, with backing from the United States, are also trying to establish themselves. The Ukraine with its strong Chassidic associations is seeing a revival of religious interest and activity.

Hungary has the largest and best organised Jewish community of all the former Soviet bloc countries. Poland has very few Jews but is trying to preserve its Jewish heritage. So too is the Czech Republic and to a lesser extent Slovakia and Romania. All these communities are benefiting from Jewish philanthropic investment, particularly from the United States.

## THE FAR EAST AND THE SOUTHERN HEMISPHERE

Indian Jewry has now almost entirely transferred to Israel, although there are still some small traces of previously ancient and proud communities dating back thousands of years. There are small, more recently arrived Jewish communities in Thailand and Hong Kong.

The largest Jewish community in the southern hemisphere used to be South Africa, strongly Zionist and committed to Jewish education. It still has a strong Jewish presence with schools and communal institutions. It too has a very strong Charedi element and a powerful Lubavitch presence. It has survived the transition from apartheid and is still active and powerful. But over the years, many South African Jews have emigrated to Canada, America, Britain, and above all to Australia where they have enriched and strengthened an already strong and well-established Jewish life mainly in Sydney and Melbourne and right across the continent.

## FUNDAMENTALISM

As with all religions Judaism, wherever it is, is currently experiencing a polarisation between fundamentalist and liberal wings. There is no serious political fundamentalism in Judaism. Only a small group of settlers in Israel use religion as a justification for their political positions. But theoretical fundamentalism is a very powerful force in Judaism today.

Some of the reasons for this are specific. The horror of the Holocaust had a deep psychological impact on many Jews. Some tried to escape the heritage that marked them out as victims by assimilating and hiding their Jewish roots. Others were determined not to grant Hitler a posthumous victory by making sure that Judaism would not disappear; they felt that the only response was to defiantly ensure Jewish survival and continuity.

The Charedi community probably suffered proportionally more than any other sector of Jewish life and so the determination of its survivors was that much more powerful. All the more so since the Eastern European Chassidic world already had a defensive mindset that simply ignored external values and was stubbornly committed to creating and sustaining its own way of life.

Those Charedi Jews who were lucky enough to get to America or Israel before the War and those who survived it responded to the catastrophe by turning inwards to focus entirely on survival. This determination was driven by a conviction that if modern, cultured society could produce the Nazis and if the world could stand by and let the Holocaust happen then there could be nothing of value in it. Similarly, if 2,000 years of Christianity could not prevent the horror emerging from the heart of Christendom, then Christianity too could not be a religion to engage with. The simple fundamentalist religion of the Charedi community enabled it to pursue its own agenda. With its vibrant birth rate and a willingness to make sacrifices in pursuit of its goals, it was helped by the post-war expansion of social welfare and family support. Although many Charedi Jews were successful in building up wealth after the War, it was this state support that also played an essential role in enabling the Charedi community with its very large families to flourish.

A feature that characterises fundamentalism in Judaism is an absolute commitment to traditional texts. This is not to be confused with Protestant fundamentalism in the way that biblical texts are taken literally, but more in terms of the absolute authority of traditional sources and rabbinic interpretation of them. Since the fourth-century fixing of the calendar according to the start of the world 5,764 years ago, Jewish fundamentalism rejects geological and archaeological evidence of much earlier dates. This is related to the belief that secular, non-religious values are false and dangerous. So evidence of the unreliability of carbon dating, changes in scientific theories, new discoveries that invalidate earlier assumptions are all used to refute anything that challenges traditional views. In this the anti-Darwin campaign of Christianity is very similar. Added to this is the belief that secular society is corrupt, and that pornography, crime, drugs and promiscuity all evidence the failure of secular society to establish moral standards. Ironically, unlike some Christian denominations, the Charedi world does not object to using the fruits of modern technology and scientific research.

Another feature of fundamentalism is the conviction that over time, spiritually speaking, generations have declined. There has been a reduction both in authority and in spiritual greatness. In part this is a response to Darwinism. However, even in the Talmud one finds the idea that previous generations were greater than the current ones. This is not just a matter of being closer to the original revelation, but a deep conviction that the level of human spirituality was in general higher and that physical capacities and resistance were stronger then too.

The result is that there is great reluctance to override earlier decisions even when there are good legal grounds. This in turn leads to a one-way incremental rise in strictness as a validation of religious authenticity.

Authority becomes essential as a method of social and political control. As most Charedi communities are dependent on the 'pork barrel' version of political reality, the ability of its leadership to deliver votes is crucial to their material survival. To ensure obedience in all matters, including electoral, religious leaders are seen to have greater measures of wisdom and inspiration. This then adds to their already established superhuman powers and they are turned to on all matters of personal concern. In other words, authority moves from text and source more to personal leadership. This was once the preserve of the Chassidic leadership, but it has now extended throughout the Charedi world.

The term 'fundamentalist' is highly controversial. One needs to distinguish between theoretical fundamentalism and political fundamentalism. Judaism has always had a strong theoretical fundamentalist strain. It has always defended its texts and its traditions in the face of theological or scientific assault. Yet at no time since the uprisings against Ancient Rome has there ever been political fundamentalism in Judaism. On the contrary, the Orthodox world has always tended to accommodate. The sort of extreme activism one sees in Islam has not occurred significantly in Judaism.

Yet it is theoretical fundamentalism that is and has been a major factor in Jewish survival. This shows no sign of reducing, on the contrary. During the immediate post-war period all Charedi institutions were essentially inward-looking, but slowly during the Sixties and Seventies many of them began to develop wings of their movements that were evangelical, directed of course towards other Jews rather than towards the outside world. This has attained a measure of success. However, in terms of numbers those leaving Judaism are far greater. This is another reason for the Charedi preoccupation with quality rather than quantity.

Fundamentalism also lays greater emphasis on the behavioural rather than the abstract. This is probably why Judaism has survived so well under so many different cultures and societies and in so many different parts of the world. Cultural differences are very powerful and Jews easily adopt the attitudes and conventions of their host societies. But wherever one lives and under whatever regime, the daily actions of living are similar. The behavioural customs and laws of Jewish life combined with the common language of prayer and study have ensured that a common thread unites.

Modern Orthodoxy differs not so much in its commitment to Halacha but on two issues. Firstly, it accepts that there is value in other cultures and in secular education. Secondly, it believes that is acceptable to challenge the authority of leaders on matters that go beyond the specifically halachic. Although Modern Orthodoxy appears to be ceding authority to the Charedi world and its synagogues are becoming centres of a social Judaism that avoids theological dispute, it is nevertheless thriving in academe.

# Chapter 9

# Judaism: The Future

According to the Talmud, after the destruction of the Temple prophecy ended and the gift was given to fools. So at best this chapter is an attempt to read trends and to extrapolate. Only someone unaware of the strength of Orthodox life around the different communities of the Jewish world today could possibly be pessimistic about the future of Judaism.

Yet if there are barely twelve million Jews in the world today and in many communities the marriage out rate runs at fifty per cent, how can Judaism possibly survive given these figures? The answer is that there are other strict religious denominations that have survived with even fewer numbers. When it comes to matters of faith, it is quality not quantity that counts.

## CHAREDI JUDAISM

Defying logic, Orthodoxy, in its Charedi forms is expanding, its institutions overflowing and its mood triumphalist. All predictions of its demise have failed. In this it is similar to the successful charismatic movements and family churches in Christianity that are more dynamic than the established churches, and to the resurgence in Islamic religious practice in the West. Indeed fundamentalist religion seems to be the mode and there seem to be no good reasons as to why this should change. In a polarised world, the stronger the pull towards libertarianism, the stronger is the counter-tendency. One is reminded of Victorian England in which the tremendous advances in science were counterbalanced by the powerful attraction of the Rosicrucians.

In a competitive insecure world, intense religious communities offer the reassurance many people need. For these reasons I can see no diminution in the growth of the Charedi world.

The biggest problem that faces them is a financial one. With such a massive birth rate and with their reluctance to engage in secular study, the question of how future generations will finance themselves is a major concern. However, attitudes are changing subtly, particularly in America where Charedi communities are increasingly encouraging its members to look for ways and means of supporting themselves and their families. Meanwhile charitable giving is such a strong element in Charedi communities that they appear to be managing better than the cynics predicted. Although there is some evidence of attrition, the remarkable success of a quasi-tribal world to retain and care for its weak as well as its strongest members seems guaranteed to flourish, even if as an anachronism in the modern world.

One would like to think that as the Charedi world becomes more confident in its survival, it might open up and become more outward looking and even amenable to change. There are no signs of this happening on an ideological level. Nevertheless, in many parts of the world one will now find Charedi men attending concerts, sports events and mixing in gentile society much more freely than in the past.

However, a Charedi life does not suit the majority of Jews. It seems to me that it is unlikely that anything more than a vociferous and vibrant minority will accept the rigours of a confined and limiting lifestyle. Furthermore, Jews who want to think for themselves will have difficulty with the naïve and simplistic Charedi world outlook. Anyone genuinely interested in either philosophy or theology, or indeed looking at the world scientifically, will find a Charedi position insufficient. The lure of a Charedi position is that it offers a closed and secure certainty. It offers a warm protective environment even if one has to sacrifice individuality. It is tough enough to be well educated in one culture, let alone two. How many Jews will want to juggle two worlds?

Nevertheless, one of the growth areas in Judaism is the outreach movement. A number of Charedi organisations, particularly those with American roots, have set up quite professional and, in a limited way, successful outreach organisations that are attracting a significant number of youngsters to a Charedi lifestyle. In the past it was Lubavitch Chassidism that was most closely identified with internal missionary activity; nowadays and in the future, it will be one amongst many.

## MODERN ORTHODOX

The most threatened position in Orthodoxy seems to be that of the middle ground, which combines a commitment to Torah with an involvement with modern society not just on a utilitarian level but on a cultural one as well. In general, those in the middle ground, who are often referred to as Modern Orthodox and who feel uncomfortable with either extreme, are faced with two choices. They can allow the Western influence to predominate and move towards the Reform communities, or they can opt for a more intense expression of Judaism and move to the right. This polarisation will increasingly represent the reality of the Jewish world.

One can find a counterbalance to this polarisation in academia. The academic world protects the intellectual from interference in a way that community rabbis and leaders are not. Throughout the Jewish and non-Jewish academic world, religiously committed Jews of great ability and increasing number are combining their Jewish practice with open intellectual enquiry and innovation. The spin-off from this is that in centres such as Jerusalem and New York, innovative yet traditional communities thrive and their influence appears to be increasing.

If there is one really bright spot in the Jewish intellectual firmament, it is this and all the evidence points towards its strengthening. It is always bolstered by a degree of fall-off from the Charedi world and, from the other direction, those *BaaLei Teshuva*, returnees, who want a more demanding and all-embracing religious life. A small number of its members, who become interested in academic study and yet remain religiously committed, bring new infusions of talent. The mainstream rabbinate in Israel is showing increasing willingness to listen and even innovate to meet the needs of those Jews who, while committed to Halacha, want to see progress. All the signs are that this will continue to be the case.

## CONSERVATIVE JUDAISM

The Conservative movement is still strong numerically in North America, but it is embattled in Israel and exists in very small numbers elsewhere. It is torn between its own left wing, which expresses a completely egalitarian and flexible attitude to Jewish law, and its own traditionalist right wing. It lacks the features that make the Charedi community vibrant, and it also lacks the freedom that allows the Reform movement to appeal to marginal Jews or those Jews who feel more acculturated in a Western environment. The Conservative movement shares the difficulties of Modern Orthodoxy in finding itself unable to offer certainties on the one hand or indulgence on the other. Although I would not predict its demise, I am not sanguine about it increasing its influence in the Jewish world.

## REFORM

Reform Judaism has not succeeded in replacing more traditional expressions of Judaism, just as one might argue that Protestantism has not replaced Catholicism. It offers a home for Jews who find tradition too restrictive and it is a home, in particular, for Jews who have married out of Judaism. In addition, Jews who find themselves excluded by some of the limitations of religious law are welcomed into Reform communities.

On the one hand, Reform is coming back to tradition and yet, on the other, it will only survive if it offers a serious alternative to traditional Judaism. At worst, it will be a port of call on the way out of Judaism. At best, it will offer an ethical counterbalance to a ritualised Orthodoxy. If it simply stays where it is as a westernised variation on a Jewish theme, it will find it harder and harder to distinguish itself from other liberal traditions.

The Reform communities are particularly important in that they spearhead the encounter with other religions. They involve themselves in wider ethical and social issues and, above all, they offer a home within Judaism for those either excluded by the Orthodox or who find themselves unable to accept Orthodox ideology. But from them, I do not see any innovative religious expression emerging.

## SECULAR ALTERNATIVES

The majority of Jews around the world are secular in practice if not ideolog-ically. For most of them Judaism is a social phenomenon rather than a spiritual one. This is why I cannot see a secular ideology emerging to offer a theoretical framework for Jewish identity. Communitarianism seems to me to offer a solution to the human dimension and to an emotional identification with Israel in the nationalist sense. If fundamentalists of different religions share more core values with fundamentalists of other religions, the same holds true of secular Jews who, *pace* anti-Semitism, share more with secular-ists of other faiths. Anti-Semitism and anti-Zionism have indeed affected secular Jews of late, but I see this as negative identification rather than positive.

Zionism has failed to offer anything other than simple nationalism. Originally it was predominantly a secular movement. Now Zionism, as an ideology, is being sustained primarily by the religious Zionists. Israelis abroad have tended to assimilate quickly into the host society. In Israel today there is much talk of the Death of Zionism or post-Zionism. Most secular Israeli youngsters share more with American pop culture than they do with Charedi Jews. If peace were to come to the Middle East, I believe a left-wing or liberal Jew would soon find more common ground with a secular or liberal Palestinian than either would with their own fundamentalists.

The Holocaust emerged after an initial period of forced silence as a powerful cohesive factor. But it, too, has lost its draw as the generation of Holocaust survivors diminishes and young people respond less to a negative perception of history than to a positive one.

Many young Israelis, as well as Americans, have been drawn to eastern meditational practices. A new generation in Israel in particular now tries to integrate eastern practices into their expression of Judaism. Hence the increasing attraction of Kabballah. Kabbalah has within its tradition many of the practices associated nowadays with the East. Kabbalah offers an expres-sion of Jewish spirituality that allows a great deal of personal experimentation and has maintained its tradition of being beyond rabbinic control and main-stream authority, which is so disliked by many young Jews nowadays. It also offers a New Age, astrological dimension of Judaism that appeals to the modern trend for simple, immediate answers to complex issues. In Israel, in particular, there is evidence of a serious rise in the numbers wanting to develop a mystical, more Eastern brand of Judaism. But unless the initial taste leads to a more intensive encounter with the religious source of Kabbalah, it will be no more than a passing fad.

Originally Chassidism set out to meet precisely these needs. Over the centuries, however, it has changed from being a radical and a revolutionary movement based on meritocratic leadership, charisma and inspiration into a fossilised, dynastic movement for conformity and control. New expressions of spirituality are unlikely to emerge there.

## A NEW KIND OF JUDAISM

The late Professor Gershom Scholem argued that Judaism has always gone through 500-year periods of reinvention or revival. Approximately 500 years after the Judean State was established, it was destroyed and the Babylonian exile influenced the development of Judaism. Five hundred years later, the destruction of Jerusalem and the Temple created a new reality. Another 500 years saw the completion of the Talmud and the emergence of the West. Five hundred years later came the Golden Age of Spain together with the emergence of Kabbalah and the flowering of Western European authorities. Five hundred years later, the Spanish Exile led to the flourishing of the great Safed centre, which in turn led to the Chassidic movement. Five hundred years on and the State of Israel helped spearhead a religious and cultural revival.

Scholem has another theory. It is that formal religious authority acts over time to alienate people from spiritual ecstasy and a closeness to nature. Mystical revolutions take place in order to re-establish a spiritual relationship with God and the world that gets lost in the formality of conformity. Given the conformity now of the Chassidic world, we should be due for a new revolution. Where will it come from?

It is unlikely to emerge from the Charedi world. The Chassidic movements require absolute obedience to their rebbes. If anything, the rebbes themselves encourage their followers to root out any signs of insurrection. Even when Chassidim disagree in private, they will not express this in public. A similar mood prevails in the Mitnaged world of the Yeshivot. The Rosh Yeshiva has almost divine authority. Conformity in everything from dress to ideology is aggressively imposed. Even in the lay synagogues and shtiebels disagreement is personal and not organised. Theological debate is suppressed in favour of social control. The dynamism of the Charedi world is entirely directed inwards and focused on survival, growth and obedience. Similarly, the outreach organisations of the Charedi world demand strict obedience.

Only in sections of Israeli Orthodox and neo-Orthodox society can one find new opportunities for women in Judaism, in the realms of scholarship and participation, new syntheses of mysticism and religious practice and a spirit of debate, experiment and creativity.

## INDIVIDUALISM

I believe that increasing opportunities for individualism within a halachic framework will be the hallmark of the next religious revolution. There is no biblical equivalent of individuality as opposed to national identity. Even in the Talmud there is no equivalent of our positive modern notion, except in a derogatory way.

The absence of central authority in Judaism is looked on by some as a weakness. But, in practice, it is a strength because it allows for degrees of variation. The strong centrifugal tendency is balanced by an equally strong tendency to fragment. The weakness of individualism is that it needs a community framework both to provide Jewish facilities and to express the religious dimensions of community life. It could be viewed as parasitic, but then some hangers-on in the animal world actually provide positive services for the host.

Fundamentalism offers a primitive passion; individualism offers a mature passion. Mature societies can cope with varieties within their own ranks.

Whatever happens, the fact that Judaism encourages accommodation to host societies, does not call on withdrawal but instead promotes active participation means that it is well placed to cope with modern society. Jews have been able to distil and adapt to the technological, commercial and economic features of modern society. Together with their tradition of scholarship, education and study, they have no difficulty in coping with the modern world. Yet they are able to bifurcate and live in two worlds, their religious world that looks to the past and their economic world that looks to the future.

## OTHER RELIGIONS

There was a time when I was convinced that Judaism and Islam were so similar that they would come closer together. Both in their shared image of a non-representational God and in their emphasis on behaviour, Halacha or Shaaria, I felt there was much more common ground than between Judaism and Christianity.

Yet, in recent years, it seems to me that the politics, not just of the Middle East but also throughout the world where Islamic societies (rather than Islam perhaps, but the jury is out on this) are still in a state of adjustment to modernity, has created an almost impassable barrier between most Muslims and most Jews. I deeply regret this.

Just as in Catholicism, American Catholics find themselves in the vanguard of change, so perhaps American Muslims may be the first to try to change attitudes, but I see no sign of this yet. The Muslim world today is by far the greatest source of and market for anti-Semitic literature. Muslim friends in Europe complain about the influence of Wahabbi extremism, particularly on disaffected or unemployed youngsters. As Bernard Lewis has argued, its impact is divisive even within the Muslim world. I would like to think that rapprochement on more than an individual level may emerge in the future.

The expression 'Judaeo-Christianity' is a contradiction in terms and misleading, if not meaningless. Despite the origins of Christianity, the differences between Greece and Jerusalem are too profound to allow for comparison. The Catholic Church has dramatically changed its public position since John XXIII began to reassess attitudes to Jews and Judaism. The present Pope, too, has played his part. But old attitudes are still to be found throughout the Catholic Church and the good intentions of much of the leadership have still not filtered down far enough. Indeed the hopes for a convergence between Catholicism and Protestantism have been disappointed and show no signs of happening, so there can be even less chance of other totally separate religions coming together. In America, in particular, the Catholic Church and the Charedi communities have forged a close working relationship on common goals and issues, even though there is absolutely no theological dialogue. In Britain the Charedi world shows great expertise in working with all sections of its communities, including Muslims and left-wing groups, for political ends. This is bound to continue and gain momentum.

Evangelical Christianity has proved to be the most sympathetic of the Protestant churches to Jews. It is arguable how much of this is to suit their theological agenda. The World Council of Churches has identified so whole-heartedly with the Palestinian cause that there is little contact with Judaism. Nevertheless, the relationship between Judaism and Christianity is probably better and more positive today than at any time in their shared history.

Relations between Judaism and Eastern religions have never suffered from the blight that the common cradle has imposed in the West. On the contrary, much of Buddhism is attractive to many Jews who now discover that much of the Buddhist holistic approach to life can be found in medieval Jewish mystical writings that were suppressed by the rationalism in Judaism.

Although our human perspective is limited, I am optimistic about the future relationship of the world's religions and I see greater convergence rather than separation. The common ground far exceeds the divisions that, as I have tried to show, are more cultural and concerned with different ways of reaching similar goals. The challenge of religions will be to stop the inter-necine squabbles that dishonour them and harm humanity and to work together to produce a more spiritual and harmonious universe.

However close in political terms the world becomes in the future, cultural and religious differences will remain. This is the nature and positive feature of human life. The European Union has not weakened cultural differences and although American commercial culture is global, increasingly it has had to come to terms with cultural differences. So I see no mergers or extinctions, but I do believe that the human need for religion will increase rather than decrease.

As religions increasingly retreat from trying to answer all the problems of the universe and relinquish their monopoly of knowledge and power, they concentrate on offering a framework for living, solace in an increasingly pressurised world and a spiritual dimension. Predictions of their demise are premature and as long as each one offers its own strong cultural manifestation of worship, I can see no possibility or even need for mergers.

# Glossary

| | |
|---|---|
| Aggadata | the section within the Talmud covering traditions, including folklore, folk medicine, and traditions of a historical and social nature, magic and the interpretation of dreams. |
| Agunah | a wife who cannot remarry because her husband has not given her a religious divorce. |
| Am HaAretz | the ordinary peasant or ignoramus. |
| Amida | literally 'a prayer said standing'; daily communal prayer. |
| Arba Kanfot | the four-cornered garment with fringes. |
| Arba'a minim | the four kinds of plants used as part of celebrations on Succot. |
| Aron | a container or 'Ark' in which the scrolls of the Torah are kept. |
| Ashkenazim | those who follow the customs of Central and Eastern European Jewry. |
| Av Beth Din | the head of the court in Judea, a position parallel to the academic head in Babylon the Reysh Metivta. Nowadays the head of a Jewish religious court. |
| Aveyra | sin (derived from the word for 'turning off the path'). |
| Avon | sin (derived from the word 'to be missing something'). |
| Baal Shem | literally 'having a name'; generic term indicating someone who had special, usually kabbalistic powers of healing. More specifically, the name of the founder of Chassidism. |
| BaaLei Teshuva | Jews 'returning' to religious practice. |
| Bar Mitzvah | celebration to mark coming of age of boys at 13. |
| Bat Mitzvah | female version of the Bar Mitzvah. |
| Batim | literally 'Houses'; boxes containing the tefillin. |
| Behab | fast-days after Succot and Pesach. |
| Beracha | blessing. |
| Beraitot | texts contemporaneous with but not included in the Mishna. |

| | |
|---|---|
| Beth Din | court of law. |
| Beth HaKnesset | the House of Gathering. Synagogue. |
| Beth midrash | a study house, can also function as a synagogue. |
| Bima | platform or table from which the Torah is read. |
| Brit | circumcision (literally 'The Covenant'). |
| Cappel, yarmulke or kippa | headgear. |
| Chalaf | sharp knife used in ritual slaughter. |
| Chalitza | relinquishing responsibility; the ceremony to waive Yibum, also a form of divorce. |
| Challuka | handouts, charity. |
| Chametz | Leaven, usually bread, not allowed on Passover. |
| Chanukah | festival to commemorate the Hasmonean re-dedication of the Temple. |
| Chanukia | eight-branched Chanukah candelabrum. |
| Charedi | literally 'Trembling before God', the term the Ultra-Orthodox world now prefers to be known as. |
| Charoset | sweet paste of nuts, wine and apples or dates eaten at Passover. |
| Chassidism (Chassidic) | 18th-century movement of the Pious, founded by Baal Shem Tov. |
| Chazan | originally an official of the synagogue, who then became the Cantor. |
| Cheder yichud | the room of intimacy; where the bridegroom and bride go after the marriage ceremony. |
| Chevra Kaddisha | after death the body is handed to this group, the 'holy society', to be washed and dressed in white shrouds and buried. |
| Cheyt | sin (derived from the word used to 'miss the mark). |
| Chillul HaShem | desecrating God's name. |
| Chok | ritual law without a rational explanation. |
| Chol HaMoed | the festive weekdays during the Passover festival. |
| Chumash | literally 'The Five' as in *Five Books of Moses*; the printed version of the Torah. |
| Chuppa | the ceremony of marriage. |
| Dayan | Judge. |
| Emunah | firmness of resolve or belief. |
| Eretz Yisrael | Land of Israel. |
| Erusin | binding commitment based on conjugality. |
| Eruv | literally 'merger', a legal device which arranges for different areas to be combined into a single domain or different holy days to be merged into one. |

| | |
|---|---|
| Ervah | nakedness, sexual immorality. |
| Gabbaey Tsedaka | charity officers. |
| Gehenna | hell. |
| Gemara | there were two Gemeras, a Jerusalem and a Babylonian; these discussions on the Mishna, together with the Mishna itself, were given the general name of the Talmud. |
| Geonim and the Saboraim | the heads of the major Baylonian academies after the Talmud. |
| Geonim | of Babylon during the post-talmudic era, the highest authority in Judaism until first millennium CE. |
| Ger Toshav | a non Jew living amongst Jews in the Land of Israel accorded civil rights. |
| Ger Tsedek | the righteous stranger, a convert to Judaism. |
| Get | a bill of divorce. |
| Geulah | redemption. |
| Goldene Medinah | Yiddish for The Golden State, the United States of America. |
| Haftarah | a reading from the prophets in synagogues on Sabbaths. |
| Haggadah | the book that contains the service for the Seder Night, the first night of Passover. |
| Halacha | the corpus of Jewish Law, covering the complete gamut of personal, communal and national life. |
| Hallel | special selection of joyful psalms, used in prayers on biblical festivals. |
| Haskallah | the enlightenment, a late 18th-century movement to encourage secular learning. |
| Havdala | ceremony of 'dividing' the sacred and the profane at the end of Shabbat. |
| Heter Isska | permission to trade; a mechanism of avoiding interest laws. |
| Hoshaa (or Yeshua) | salvation. |
| Hoshanna Rabba | 'the great salvation'; the last of the intermediary days during the Succot festival. |
| Kaballah | literally, 'the received tradition'; the body of mystical, esoteric studies. |
| Kabbalat Shabbat | 'receiving Shabbat'; additional psalms and songs, to welcome in the Shabbat at the Friday evening service. |
| Kaddish | a prayer, meaning 'sanctification'; it is not a special mourners' prayer but is recited by mourners at services. |

| | |
|---|---|
| Karpas | herbs dipped in saltwater and eaten at Passover. |
| Keriah | a symbolic tear in one's clothes as a sign of mourning. |
| Keriat HaTorah | reading from the Torah. |
| Ketuba | marriage contract. |
| Kiddush | dedication of the Shabbat over a cup of wine. |
| Kiddush HaShem | sanctifying God's Name or witness. |
| Kinot | medieval poems of mourning read on ninth of Av. |
| Knesset | the Israeli parliament. |
| Kol nidrei | literally meaning 'all vows', a special declaration in the evening service on Yom Kippur. |
| Kri ketiv | according to the Massoretic tradition, meaning 'read and written', in which some words and letters are written differently from the way they are read. |
| Leumi | nationalist, applied to movements and institutions in Israel. |
| Ma'amad | while those who could went up to Jerusalem, the local community gathered in their synagogues and studied what was happening in Jerusalem. The ma'amad was the term used to connect the local Israelites studying with those standing by in Jerusalem, related to the Mishmar, the rota of Levites and Priests. |
| Maariv | evening prayer. |
| Maaser sheni | one of the obligatory biblical tithes. |
| Mamzerim | children born to a sexual union forbidden in the Torah. Not the same as Western illegitimacy. |
| Maror | bitter herbs used in Passover meal. |
| Mashiach | Messiah, literally anointed priest or king. |
| Masorti | name used in some countries for Jews who are active members of the Conservative movement. |
| Matzah | unleavened bread. Obligatory on Passover. |
| Mayim acharonim | 'final waters'; custom of washing one's fingertips at the end of a meal. |
| Mazal | Astrology or luck. |
| Melaveh malka | literally 'following the queen'; a Saturday night festive meal in Chassidic circles. |
| Menorah | seven-branched candelabrum. |
| Metivtot or yeshivot | Jewish talmudic academies. |
| Mezuzah | the scroll placed on doors of Jewish homes to indicate their dedication to the Torah. |
| midrash | the section within and beyond the Talmud covering exegetical and homiletical interpretation of scriptures; also the vehicle of what one might call |

|                        |                                                                                                            |
|------------------------|------------------------------------------------------------------------------------------------------------|
|                        | theological discussion and preaching to the wider audiences.                                               |
| Mikvah                 | the ritual bath.                                                                                            |
| Milchemet Mitzvah      | an obligatory war.                                                                                          |
| Milchemet Reshut       | an optional war.                                                                                            |
| Mincha                 | afternoon prayer.                                                                                           |
| Minyan                 | literally the 'number', ten adult men, the notion of community for public prayer.                          |
| Mishmar                | traditionally ascribed to King David, the priests and Levites were divided administratively into 'clans' called a 'watch' to serve in the Temple. |
| Mishna                 | written compilation of the Oral Law in the second century.                                                 |
| Mishpatim              | Jewish civil laws.                                                                                          |
| Mitnagdim              | the opponents of Chassidism (led by Gaon of Vilna).                                                        |
| Mitzvah                | General term for a religious command.                                                                       |
| Mitzvot                | The Commandments.                                                                                           |
| Mohel                  | a circumciser.                                                                                              |
| Motzi                  | a blessing derived from the Hebrew wording that thanks God for 'bringing bread from the earth'.            |
| Musaf                  | additional service on Shabbat and Festivals.                                                               |
| Musaf                  | an additional prayer.                                                                                       |
| Nasi                   | the head of the community in the Land of Israel, a position parallel to the Exilarch in Babylon.          |
| Navi                   | prophet.                                                                                                    |
| Nefesh, ruach and neshama | soul.                                                                                                    |
| Neilah                 | literally 'the closing of the gates', the last service on Yom Kippur.                                      |
| Nida                   | a woman during her period.                                                                                  |
| Niglah                 | the revealed knowledge of the Torah, including the biblical and talmudic texts and all aspects of Halacha. |
| Nissuin,               | marriage.                                                                                                   |
| Nistar                 | 'the Secret body of knowledge' was the term used for esoteric, mystical study, eventually known as Kaballah. |
| Nisuch HaMayim         | poured out water, forming part of the ceremonies asking God for rain during the Succot festival. Of prophetic origin. |
| Omer                   | the first sheaf of the first barley harvest, whose dedication marks the start of the agricultural year at the start of Passover. |

| | |
|---|---|
| Perushim | Pharisees. |
| Pesach | Passover. |
| Pesha | sin (derived from the word 'to falter'). |
| Piyutim | Medieval religious poems read during Festivals particularly the High Holy Days. |
| Rav | literally 'master' or 'teacher'. |
| Rebbe | heads of dynasties a title reserved only for Chassidic masters. |
| Retsuot | black leather straps, used to keep the batim of the Tefillin in place. |
| Reysh Galuta | The Exilarch of Babylonian Jewry who was the community head descended from the Davidic line. |
| Reysh Metivta | the academic head in Babylon. |
| Rosh Chodesh | 'Festival' of the new moon. |
| Rosh Hashanna | the New Year. |
| Sanhedrin | the Supreme Court of Law. |
| Sechach | roofing of the Succah. |
| Seder | main meal on the first night(s) of Passover. |
| Seudat mitzvah | a celebratory meal after circumcision. |
| Sephardim | Jews following the oriental traditions. |
| Sephirot | the ten emanations (Kabbalah). |
| Seudat mitzva | a meal to celebrate any religious event. |
| Seudat shlishit | the third meal on Shabbat, after the afternoon service. |
| Shabbat | The Sabbath, the Seventh day. |
| Shacharit | morning prayer. |
| Shalom Zachar | the 'welcoming of the male', a celebration held on the Friday night before circumcision. |
| Shavuot | Pentecost. |
| She'elot Uteshuvot | 'Questions and Answers' the way Jewish Law develops through 'learned opinions' which are written, distributed and discussed amongst experts acknowledged for their mastery of traditional sources. |
| Shechina | the Divine Presence. |
| Shechita | ritual slaughter. |
| Shema | the most important Jewish confession, recited twice daily. |
| Shemini Atzeret | 'the congregation of the eighth day'; the final day or days of Succot. |
| Shemona Esreh | eighteen blessings, also known as the Amida. |
| Sheva brachot | the seven blessings in the marriage ceremony. |
| Shevarim | the sound of sadness and mourning blown on the |

|                        | Shofar.                                                                                      |
|------------------------|---------------------------------------------------------------------------------------------|
| Shiva                  | seven-day mourning period (literally 'seven').                                               |
| Shofar                 | the ram's horn blown on Rosh Hashanna.                                                       |
| Shtiebel               | little house in Yiddish; the prayer/study house.                                            |
| Simchat Torah          | 'the rejoicing of the law'; the final day of Succot in the Diaspora.                        |
| Sofer                  | scribe who writes the scroll of the Torah.                                                   |
| Succah                 | temporary hut used on the festival of Succot.                                               |
| Succot                 | Festival of Tabernacles.                                                                     |
| Talit                  | prayer shawl.                                                                                |
| Tefilla                | prayer.                                                                                      |
| Tefillin               | phylacteries.                                                                                |
| Tekia                  | the sound blown on the Shofar to announce a meeting.                                         |
| Teruah                 | the sound of alarm blown on the Shofar.                                                      |
| Teshuva                | repentance.                                                                                  |
| Tikkun Leil Shavuot    | literally 'the order (programme) of the eve of Shavuot'.                                     |
| Tikkun olam            | the responsibility to 'improve the world'.                                                   |
| Torah                  | general term that applies both to the Five Books of Moses and the general corpus of Jewish Law, custom and interpretation. |
| Tosefta                | additional oral law texts not included in the Talmud.                                        |
| Tsitsit                | the fringes on the four-cornered garment.                                                    |
| Urim and Thumim        | the twelve stones representing the Twelve Tribes on the breastplate of the High Priest during the First Temple period. |
| Vaad Arbaa Aratsot     | Committee of the Four Lands, which in effect governed the Jews of Eastern Europe from the sixteenth until the end of the eighteenth century. |
| Wissenchaft            | the academic, scientific study of Judaism.                                                   |
| Yibum                  | the Levirate marriage. The obligation to marry a dead brother's wife when there are no children. |
| Yom Kippur             | Day of Atonement.                                                                            |
| Zadokim                | Saduccees.                                                                                   |
| Zimun                  | the ceremony of 'inviting' each other to say grace.                                         |
| Zohar                  | the great mystical work that is both a commentary on the Torah and a series of lectures on mystical themes. |

# Bibliography

General History
Salo W. Baron, *A Social and Religious History of the Jews*, Columbia University
    Press, New York
Paul Johnson, *A History of the Jews*, Harper Collins, London
Martin Gilbert, *The Routledge Atlas of Jewish History*, Routledge, London
Cecil Roth, *A History of the Jews*, Schocken Books, New York

Specific History
Howard M. Sachar, *History of the Jews in America*, Random House/Vintage,
    New York
H. Zimmels, *Ashkenazim and Sepharadim*, Ktav, New Jersey
Y. Baer, *A History of the Jews in Christian Spain*, Jewish Publication Society of
    America, Philadelphia
Solomon Zeitlin, *The Rise and Fall of the Judean State*, Jewish Publication
    Society of America, Philadelphia
Cecil Roth, *Essays and Portraits in Anglo-Jewish History*, Jewish Publication
    Society of America, Philadelphia

Zionism
Arthur Hertzberg, *The Zionist Idea – A Historical Analysis and reader*, Jewish
    Publication Society of America, Philadelphia
Joan Peters, *From Time Immemorial: The Origins of the Arab–Jewish Conflict
    over Palestine*, Harper Collins, New York
Shlomo Avineri, *The Making of Modern Zionism*, Basic Books, New York
Walter Laquer, *The History of Zionism*

Archaeology
Jonathan N. Tubb, *Canaanites*, British Museum Press, London
D. Winton Thomas, *Documents of Old Testament Times*, Nelson, London
Israel Finkelstein, *The Bible Unearthed*, Simon & Schuster, New York

Bible Studies
Yechezkel Kaufman, *The Religion of Israel*, University of Chicago Press, Chicago
Umberto Cassutto, *Genesis*, Magnus Press, Hebrew University, Jerusalem

Talmud
Ephraim Urbach, *The Sages*, Magnus Press, Hebrew University, Jerusalem

## Mysticism

Gershom Scholem, *Major Trends in Jewish Mysticism*, Schocken, New York

Aryeh Kaplan, *Meditation and Kabbalah*, Red Wheel/Weiser, Maine

Moshe Idel, *Messianic Mystics*, Yale University Press

Moshe Idel, *Absorbing Perfections – Kabbalah and Interpretation*, Yale University Press

## Theology

Abraham J Heschel, *God in Search of Man*, Noonday Books, New York

Eliezer Berkovits, *Major Themes in Modern Philosophies of Judaism*, Ktav, New Jersey

## Jewish Law

Isaac Klein, *A Guide to Jewish Religious Practice*, Jewish Publication Society of America, Philadelphia

Shubert Spero, *Morality, Halakha and the Jewish Tradition*, Ktav, New Jersey

Adin Steinzaltz, *A Guide to Jewish Prayer*, Schocken, New York

Loius Jacobs, *A Tree of Life: Diversity, Flexibility and Creativity in Jewish Law*, Littman Library of Jewish Civilisation, Oxford University Press

Hayim Halevy Donin, *To be a Jew: A Guide to Jewish Observance in Contemporary Life*, Basic Books, New York

Hayim Halevy Donin, *To Pray as a Jew: A Guide to the Prayer Book and Synagogue Service*, Basic Books, New York

Abraham Joshua, *The Sabbath: its Meaning for Modern Man*, Farrar Strauss, New York

Maurice Lamm, *The Jewish Way in Death and Mourning*, Jonathan David, New York

## Primary Texts

J.H. Hertz, *The Pentateuch*, Soncino, London

Nosson Scherman, *Stone Edition of the Chumash the Torah*, Mesorah Publications, New York

*The Chumash*, Heritage Foundation Art Scroll, Mesorah Publications, New York

*The Tanach*, Heritage Foundation Art Scroll, Mesorah Publications, New York

Herbert Danby, trans., *The Mishna*, Yale University Press

*The Talmud*, Soncino, New York

*The Zohar*, Soncino, New York

*The Midrash*, Soncino, New York

Hayyim Nahman Bialik, *The Book of Legends (Sefer Ha-Aggadah)*, Knopf, New York

## General

*Encyclopedia Judaica*, Keter, Jerusalem, Macmillan, London

Jacob Neusner, *Encyclopedia of Judaism*, Continuum, New York

# Index

146